INDEX
ON CENSORSHIP

Yet still I hide something,
still save something.
The most strong and gallant
I will not give up to anyone.

Boris Slutsky

INDEX ON CENSORSHIP 5 1997

Volume 26 No 5 September/October 1997 Issue 178

Index on Censorship (ISSN 0306-4220) is published bi-monthly by a non-profit-making company: Writers & Scholars International Ltd, Lancaster House, 33 Islington High Street, London N1 9LH *Tel*: 0171-278 2313 *Fax*: 0171-278 1878 *Email*: indexoncenso@gn.apc.org http://www.oneworld.org/index_oc/ Index on Censorship is associated with Writers & Scholars Educational Trust, registered charity number 325003
Periodicals postage: (US subscribers only) paid at Newark, New Jersey. Postmaster: send US address changes to Index on Censorship c/o Mercury Airfreight Int/ Ltd Inc, 2323 Randolph Avenue, Avenel, NJ 07001, USA

Subscriptions 1997 (6 issues p.a.) Individuals: UK £38, US $50, rest of world £43 Institutions: UK £42, US $72, rest of world £48 Students: UK £25, US $35, rest of world £31

Funded by
THE
ARTS
COUNCIL
OF ENGLAND

The Trustees of Writers & Scholars Educational Trust would like to thank The Arts Council of England and The Stephen Spender Memorial Fund for their support for this special issue

Former Editors: Michael Scammell (1972-81); Hugh Lunghi (1981-83); George Theiner (1983-88); Sally Laird (1988-89); Andrew Graham-Yooll (1989-93)

Stephen Spender (1909-1995) poet, passionate believer in free expression
and founder of *Index on Censorship*, to whom
Banned Poetry is dedicated.

'The opposite of censorship is self-expression, which we call literature.'
— Stephen Spender writing in *Index* 1&2/1994

The editors are grateful to the many people who have helped with the
compilation of this edition. Thanks are particularly due to Abdullah al-
Udhari, Gordon Brotherston, Ruth Christie, Moris Farhi, Richard
McKane, Bill Swainson and the staff of International PEN

contents

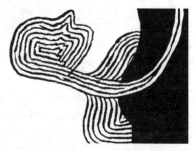

PETER PORTER & HARRIET HARVEY WOOD

Shadow worlds

A S ONCE every 24 hours each part of the world moves into and out of darkness, the human race has always regarded the antinomy of day and night as its basic evidence of existence. Consequently from the very beginnings of literature such symbolism has helped us explain our moral natures to ourselves. Those conditions of life we regard as essential to freedom and prosperity we see as open and visible, and those which are occluded, oppressive and secret we judge to be in shadow. So omnipresent and various are the metaphors of light and shade that world literature, especially that part expressed in poetry, might be summed up within this crucial opposition — God, Creator of Light and his opponent, Lucifer, Prince of Darkness; Zeus, overthrower of Chaos; Persephone, daughter of Earth trapped underground each year by Dis, God of Death; and so on. These instances are not just anthropological or theocratic: philosophy, psychoanalysis and fiction tell us of the double nature of our personalities, of the full figures we adopt in light and their shadowy opposites; of Jekyll and Hyde, Desdemona and Iago, of good and evil inexorably facing each other.

Unfortunately, the modern world scarcely permits any clear-cut division of social and political activity into light and dark. Everywhere we look there are disturbing shadows covering to a greater or lesser degree the free operations of the human spirit. The art critic's term 'chiaroscuro', an oxymoron of illumination and its shadowy contrast, is an apt emblem of the state of our diverse congregation of nations as it prepares to enter the Third Millennium. The so-called free nations are not properly free while the oppressing nations go on being truly oppressive. Many regions inhabit some sort of tenebrous middle condition. This is why *Index* has used the phrase 'shadow worlds' in the title for this issue; whatever the eclipses which contributors to these pages may have had to outface — and they can be subtle, almost self-impelled as well as directly imposed by authority — they cast a shadow over artistic expression and freedom of comment which the authors have had to take account of.

THIS special issue is dedicated to the memory of Stephen Spender, the founder of *Index* and a powerful and generous supporter of its activities everywhere in the world. Spender was primarily a poet and his concern for freedom was strongest when faced with the persecution and suppression which poetry has suffered this century. Some commentators have suggested that the censorship of poetry, both Left and Right, is a sort of warped tribute to its power. Few poets labouring under such censorship in reality would be likely to agree. Nevertheless, we might ask why intolerant rulers should read poetry so carefully in order to assess whether it has any subversive content. They don't do that in the West, our somewhat unquestioning assumption goes. Generally the West relies on a highly commercialised market to marginalise its recalcitrant voices. Obscurity and impoverishment are more familiar bogies than prison or exile. A new range of censorings, by market forces and the imposition of the lowest common denominator, has spread through countries which have thrown off the yoke of direct coercion. Many observers have remarked on the phenomenon of a burgeoning pornography industry taking the place of serious literature where originally seriousness was supported by the state. True, all too often, that support went hand in hand with state censorship, but today we may conclude that some countries have thrown the baby out with the bathwater. Now anything goes but little worthwhile is supported.

Not that censorship, direct and indirect, has gone away. We live in a climate of a thousand shadows. Western guardians of freedom, apart from being all too inclined to believe that the concept of freedom belongs to them alone, have seen censorship as endemic to Communist states. Therefore, when Communism as a world system collapsed, they expected censorship to cease to be a major problem. There are two things wrong with this assumption. Firstly, even where Communism has been replaced by apparently more beneficent regimes, the habit of enforcement has been retained — for example, Albania and several of the former states affiliated with the former Soviet Union which have reverted to rivalry among themselves and to a fierce nationalism. Secondly, the western virus of mercantilism has proved all but unconquerable in former Communist societies which have never had the chance to develop any immunity to it. Thus change in the great Eastern bloc, plus its outriders in Africa, Asia and the Caribbean, has been less than complete.

The end of the Cold War has left plenty of scope for tyranny and censorship elsewhere, most notably among regimes we categorise as right-wing or fundamentalist. A quick run-through of names is daunting enough — China, Indonesia, Burma, several Islamic countries including Saudi Arabia, Iran, Turkey, parts of South America and some Tweedledum and Tweedledee shiftings of power in Africa. Writers in these domains may be heroes one day and proscribed traitors the next. As T S Eliot put it in another context — 'Between the notion/ And the act/ Falls the Shadow.' The shadow is all too likely to be philistine as well as suspicious. Writers in these societies should presume that to write well is to put oneself up for questioning automatically.

Perhaps more difficult to chart and therefore more shadowy in its ramifications is the roll-call of non-aligned countries where everything is not well with the body politic. When political tyranny wanes it often allows other social discriminations to emerge. Religious orthodoxy, sexual intolerance, whether of women or homosexuals, racial hatred — these continue to flourish. It is because such world-wide interference still exists for writers that *Index* has devoted an issue to their stifled works, last year to fiction, this year to poets. You will discover in the following pages poems from many lands which have at some time or other been suppressed, though not necessarily for directly political reasons. Many go some way back in time though none could be called dated in an aesthetic sense. All bear witness to the refusal of the human will to be diverted from its goal, whether that goal is to tell the truth about life in the writer's country or, equally importantly, to follow some artistic impulse running counter to embattled theocratic or chauvinistic forces.

As an example of justifiable vindication, we would point to Vedat Türkali's poem 'Istanbul', written in 1944 and long outlawed in Turkey. It is now widely known in the poet's country, but its long ostracism has militated against its acceptance elsewhere.

A more extraordinary, indeed an almost unbelievable smothering, is offered its first release in the four 'suras' taken from Abdullah al-Udhari's 'Arab creation myth'. The triumph of Islam in the seventh century AD led not to the suppression of aboriginal Arabic traditions but simply to their being forgotten. The great originals of pre-Islamic poetry were swept away as if by floodwater. Where remnants of them were known they were wrongly thought to be derived from other better-known texts from the area — from the Book of Genesis for instance. Now Abdullah al-Udhari has crowned a lifetime's scholarly work by restoring to the Arab peoples an exciting part of their religious and artistic inheritance and it will never be published in its original in the Arab world. We are lucky too that he is such a fine poet; his rendition of these 'suras' into English testifies to his enlightenment and skill.

Leonid Aranzon, who died young in Leningrad, has yet to be properly reinstated in St Petersburg. Here you can read three poems of his which help establish him as one of the most gifted imaginations of the 1960s. These poems are *samizdat* in the purest sense — the times were not propitious to publication when they were written. A different kind of shadow life is exhibited in the Quechua song from Peru. Regina Harrison's English version is printed alongside the original Spanish native language macaronic poem. Here is a small step towards rescuing an indigenous culture from an overlaying one. Eliseo Diego from Cuba has never lacked recognition in his native land, and that has been true despite his not lending his pen to the Castro regime. But the world blockade of Cuba has denied him proper acceptance outside the island so that he has not had his standing confirmed among fellow Latin American poets. Our Polish poets might be justified on roughly the same score. In that country ironies tend to upset the Church and respectable society as much as they do the government.

World-famous Allen Ginsberg is represented by two characteristic poems which have not been suppressed in print form but which may not be heard on American daytime radio. The spoken word has always proved more inflammatory than the written. The same Ginsberg homosexual dithyrambs have also aroused the anathema of the Catholic Church in Poland. Poems from Kurdistan have been judged inadmissible in both Turkey and Iran. It seems that human nature frequently finds it intolerable to offer justice to minorities in its midst. •

Despite the examples above, the greater part of the verse included in this issue is once more straightforwardly unacceptable to the governments of the writers' countries. Liu Hong Bin and Yang Lian would not be allowed to publish their poetry in China today. Ken Saro-Wiwa has already paid the price of his opposition to Nigeria's rulers. Mahmoud Darwish and Adonis have not only endured the destruction of their homelands but have had to bear the fact that as exiles they cannot look for a stable readership, and are acceptable to other Arab regimes only while they follow official lines. Goran Simic's poems reflect directly what happens when a country is ransacked by civil war. The question for Simic is not so much who will print his poetry as who will read and respond to it. We also honour some of the great protesters who are departed — Osip Mandelstam and Nazim Hikmet — those whom no persecution could force to abandon their art.

We must emphasise that this is a collection of poetry, not a journalistic dossier on persecution and state malpractice. No poem has got in only because its author has suffered. We are also aware that since everything has been put into English we may be adding to the suffering of the writers. We have insisted on getting the best translations and realisations available. The essays which accompany the poems flesh out aspects of modern censorship in practice. There can be no disputing that monstrosities visited on people are more terrible than distortions inflicted on art and literature. For once, though, it is the latter we wish to draw your attention to. Art is always its own oracle and, as with jurisprudence, it may be saddled with the observation that 'hard cases make bad law'. Poets will always be hard cases and too often find no-one to speak up for them. We hope readers will be interested in this attempt to bring a few persecuted writers out of the shadows where they have been condemned to linger.

We have made every effort to trace the authors, publishers and translators of the poems. Where we have failed we can only apologise and insist that our action has been scrupulous and professional, and hindered only by difficulties of communication. Dates of composition of individual poems are given only in cases where this information has been supplied by the writer. ❏

Peter Porter was born in Australia in 1929 and has lived in London since 1951. He has published 13 collections of poetry and collaborated with the painter Arthur Boyd on four books of poems and pictures. He is also a reviewer of literature and music in journals and for the BBC. After his Collected Poems *(1983), his publications include* The Automatic Oracle *(1987),* Possible Worlds *(1989) and* The Chair of Babel *(1992). His most recent collection is* Dragons in Their Pleasant Palaces *(1997)*

Harriet Harvey Wood was born in 1934 and educated in Edinburgh. Before joining the British Council, she worked as an orchestral manager. She has written on Scottish literature, and has frequently given talks overseas on contemporary British writing and the place of literature in international cultural relations. In 1992 she was one of the Booker judges. She retired in 1994 after 14 years as Head of Literature. She was appointed OBE in 1992

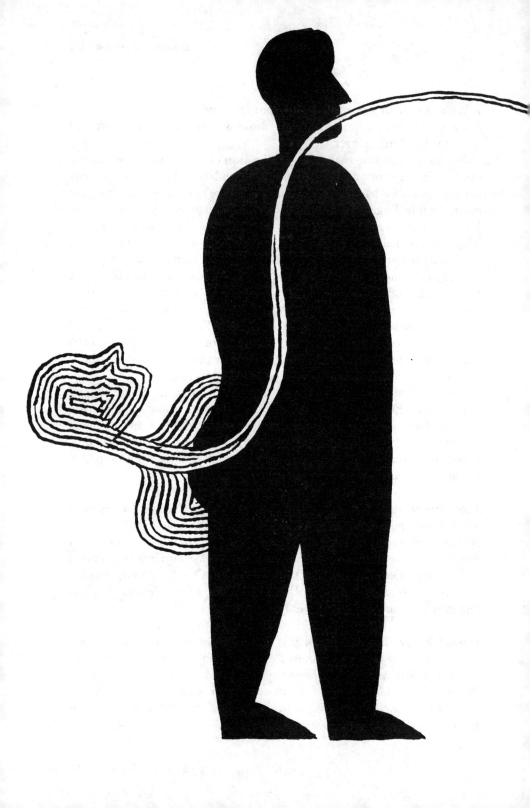

ABDULLAH AL-UDHARI

The Arab creation myth

MUSLIM theologians dub the *Jahiliyya* (pre-Islam period) as 'the age of spiritual darkness'. This misconception has over the centuries blurred our understanding not only of *Jahiliyya* but also of the Quran. The Muslim theologians seem to forget that the Quran is essentially a *Jahili* work whose language, terms of reference and message were crystal-clear to the *Jahilis*. The Muslim theologians also seem to forget that the Prophet Muhammad stressed throughout his preaching life that Islam was not a new religion but the continuation of the *Jahili Hanif* (monotheist) religion his ancestors Ibrahim (Abraham) and his son Isma'il (Ishmael) inherited from Adam and his son Hibatullah (Seth). The Prophet Muhammad regarded the *Jahilis* as monotheists who believed in Allah as the One and Only God, but who, over the centuries, distorted their faith by introducing other deities and worshipping them as intermediaries between themselves and Allah. The Prophet maintained that the introduction of the intermediary deities corrupted the original message of Ibrahim and Isma'il, which was subsequently restored by Islam.

Another group of overzealous Muslim theologians hold that Islam was a new religion with no *Jahili* connection. They have unjustifiably incorporated the *Jahili* cultural terms of reference into the Muslim lore, and because of this misleading and overzealous approach the *Jahili* heritage is seen through a Muslim perspective.

When the early Muslim exegetes interpreted the Quran they resorted to *Jahiliyya*, but instead of acknowledging the Quran's *Jahili* background they perceived the *Jahili* relevant references as echoes from other cultures like Persian, Jewish, Greek, Roman, Ethiopic and Syriac. Since most of the early Muslim exegetes were of non-Arab origin and belonged to the *Shu'ubi* (anti-Arab) intellectual movement, they claimed that the Quran was mainly influenced by their own ethnic cultures.

The Arabist scholarship of the last 200 years suppressed *Jahili* culture by dismissing it as shredded copies of other cultures, notably Jewish and Christian. The Arabists argued that the *Jahilis* were either illiterate nomads or semiliterate sedentary people who lived on the fringes of the Arabian Peninsula, had no concept of bookwriting and were incapable of producing worthwhile literature and mythology. The problem with the Arabist scholarship is that its proponents have an insufficient knowledge of the Arab language and are, therefore, in no position to read and grasp the Quran and the *Jahili* texts, let alone determine their authenticity. Further, the Arabist scholarship has overlooked the Arab and Judaeo-Christian link. If the Arab and Jewish traditions are true that Ibrahim (Abraham) was a historical figure, and was the progenitor of Isma'il (Ishmael) and Isaac, the patriarchs of the Arabs and the Jews, and that the two sons adopted their father's faith, then the Genesis lore must obviously belong to both the Arabs and the Jews. The joint ownership of the Genesis lore leads to the conclusion that an Arab Genesis exists alongside the Hebrew Genesis. The general outline of the Arab and Hebrew Genesis stories confirms this view, though the stories differ in emphasis and detail.

Contrary to the view of the Muslim theologians, the Quran exegetes and the Arabists, the *Jahiliyya* is one of the richest periods in the history of Arab civilisation. It was a spiritually and culturally fertile period whose achievements shaped and determined the course of Islam, and left an indelible mark on the imagination of the peoples who came under the influence of Islam. The *Jahilis* created a wealth of highly imaginative myths reflecting every aspect of *Jahili* life, of which the Arab creation myth is a prime example.

The Arab creation myth is a reconstruction of the *Jahili* Genesis story that has remained in fragmentary form since the advent of Islam. ❏

© *Abdullah al-Udhari*

Abdullah al-Udhari, poet, translator and literary historian, was born in Taiz, Yemen, in 1941. He grew up in a world peopled by mythological and folk heroes, kept alive by storytellers who travelled Yemen during Ramadan and on the feastdays of the prophets and saints, and, since his childhood, has been fascinated by the Arab myth of creation. He has spent over 30 years rescuing the myth and restoring it to its rightful place. He is the author of Victims of a Map *and* Modern Poetry of the Arab World

The Arab creation myth, sura 16–19

SURA SIXTEEN

The statue of man

1
Allah told the earth: 'Earth, out of your soil I will create new
Man creatures, some of whom will obey Me and others will
disobey Me. Those who obey Me will go to paradise, but those
who disobey Me will go to hell.'

2
The earth said: 'Lord, could all the new Man creatures You
will create out of my soil go to paradise?'

3
Allah said: 'Only if they all obey Me.'

4
The thought that some of the new Man creatures Allah would
create out of her soil would end up in hell so upset the earth that
she wept and wept until her face was a landscape of tearful
springs.

5
Allah called Jibreel: 'Jibreel, go down to earth and get Me a
handful of soil.'

6
Jibreel went down to earth and as he was about to scoop a
handful of soil the earth said: 'May Allah protect me if you
reduce me in size and disfigure me and let part of me end up in
hell.'

7
Jibreel was moved by the earth's invocation of Allah's

protection and returned to Allah without the soil and said:
'Lord, I haven't brought You any soil because the earth invoked
Your protection and I couldn't get myself to reduce her in size
and disfigure her and let part of her end up in hell.'

8
Allah called Mikaa'eel: 'Mikaa'eel, go down to earth and get
Me a handful of soil.'

9
Mikaa'eel went down to earth and, like Jibreel, was disarmed
by the earth's invocation of Allah's protection and returned to
Allah emptyhanded.

10
Allah called Azraa'eel: 'Azraa'eel, go down to earth and get
Me a handful of soil.'

11
Azraa'eel went down to earth and as he was about to scoop a
handful of soil the earth said: 'May Allah protect me if you
reduce me in size and disfigure me and let part of me end up in
hell.'

12
Azraa'eel, indifferent to the earth's invocation of Allah's
protection, threw back coldly: 'May Allah protect me if I
disobey His orders,' and scooped a handful of black, red and
white soil from the mountains, the wadis and the plains of the
four corners of the earth, and returned to Allah.

13
Azraa'eel said to Allah: 'Lord, here is the handful of soil You
asked for.'

14
The earth cried and prayed: 'Lord, Azraa'eel snatched a
handful of soil from me, and was indifferent to my invocation

of Your protection. Lord, tell Azraa'eel to give me back what he coldly snatched from me. Lord, help me get my soil back.'

15
Allah said to the earth: 'Calm down, it was I Who ordered Azraa'eel to get a handful of your soil. But have no fear, you will have back what was taken from you.'

16
Allah said to Azraa'eel: 'Azraa'eel, why were you indifferent to the earth when the earth invoked My protection?'

17
Azraa'eel said: 'Lord, the desire to obey Your orders and the fear of displeasing You urged me to fulfil Your orders.'

18
Allah said: 'In that case, Azraa'eel, I appoint you as the angel of death.'

19
All at once Azraa'eel's body was studded with the eyes of all living creatures, and when a living creature died, the eyes of the dead creature lost their glow and fell off Azraa'eel's body and the eyes of a newborn creature appeared in their place.

20
Jibreel soaked the threecolour soil in the deliciously fresh spring water of Ain Tasneem and kneaded it and left it for forty years until it stank and turned into mouldable clay, and out of the mouldable clay Allah shaped the Statue of Man in His Own Image with His Own Hands.

21
Allah let the cloud of worry and grief pass over the Statue of Man and release its load of worry and grief over it for forty years.

22
Allah let the cloud of joy pass over the Statue of Man and
release its load of joy over it for a year.

23
Allah left the Statue of Man to dry and harden for forty years
and then exhibited it for another forty years on the road through
which the angels travelled up and down the heavens.

24
The angels marvelled at the beauty of the face and at the height
of the Statue of Man as they had not seen anything like it
before, not even on Allah's Throne that had pictures of all His
creations.

25
The unique and imposing figure of the Statue of Man became
the talk of the seven paradises and of the seven heavens.

26
The angels who had never seen Allah reflected: 'This new
Man creature is of stinking earthly soil and we are of Divine
Light, and since we were created before all other creatures, we
are superior to them as well as to this new Man creature. Let
Allah create whatever He likes, but He will never create
creatures more noble and more perceptive than us.'

27
Allah read the angels' thoughts.

SURA SEVENTEEN

Azaazeel and the statue of man

1
Azaazeel was apprehensive about the Statue of Man, and
whenever he saw it he slapped it and kicked it and a tinkling
sound rang throughout its hollow form.

2
Sometimes Azaazeel slithered in through the Statue's mouth
and explored its hollow form before slithering out of its bottom;
and sometimes he slithered in through its bottom and slithered
out of its mouth and said to the angels: 'Don't be afraid of this
strange creature of stinking earthly soil. He is hollow and brittle
and will not last. What will you do if Allah appoints him as
your commander?'

3
The angels replied: 'We will obey Our Lord.'

4
Azaazeel was intrigued by the Statue and said to it: 'You were
not created for the sake of your potterish sound but for some
other reason.'

5
Azaazeel then said to himself: 'If Allah appoints this creature
as my commander I will disobey him, and if Allah appoints me
as his commander I will destroy him.'

6
Azaazeel pondered the hollow form of the Statue and
concluded: 'As this creature is hollow he will need food and
drink.'

7
Allah read Azaazeel's thoughts.

SURA EIGHTEEN

The expulsion of Iblees

1
Allah summoned the angels and Azaazeel to the Statue of Man,
and told them: 'I have created the Statue of Man out of earthly
soil in My Own Image with My Own Hands. Bow to the
Statue of Man who is in My Own Image.'

2
The angels said to themselves: 'We thought we were dearer to
Allah than this creature of stinking earthly soil, because we are
closer to Allah than all other creatures, and we never thought
Allah would go so far as to order us to bow to an inferior
creature.'

3
Allah read the angels' thoughts.

4
The angels bowed to the Statue of Man but not Azaazeel.

5
The angels raised their heads and when they saw Azaazeel
standing erect and looking scornfully at them they quickly
bowed their heads again.

6
Allah said to Azaazeel: 'Azaazeel, what is stopping you from
bowing to the Statue of Man I created in My Own Image with
My Own Hands?'

7
Azaazeel said: 'Lord, so this is what You look like! Lord,
what prompted You to create the Statue of Man in Your Own
Image? Is it because You miss looking at Yourself? Or is it
because You miss the company of other Allahs?'

8

Allah said: 'There are no other Allahs, nor will there ever be. I am the One and Only Allah. I am Whole and Perfect. I miss nothing.'

9

Azaazeel said: 'Lord, do You want me to worship the Statue of Man who looks like You?'

10

Allah said: 'No-one is worshipped but Me. I am the One and Only worshipped Allah.'

11

Azaazeel said: 'Lord, why then is the Statue of Man in Your Own Image?'

12

Allah said: 'You have not been summoned to question Me, but to obey My Will. Bow to the Statue of Man.'

13

Azaazeel said: 'Lord, are You aware of what You have done? By creating the Statue of Man in Your Own Image You have given him the illusion that he is a copy of You. Lord, do You want me to endorse such an illusion?'

14

Allah said: 'It is My Will you bow to the Statue of Man.'

15

Azaazeel said: 'Lord, bowing is a form of praying. Lord, do You want me to pray to the Statue of Man and endorse his divine status? Lord, as the Statue of Man is a copy of You he will be just as curious as You are. Lord, I appeal to You to think again before You slip down this precipitous curiosity.'

16

Allah said: 'I know what I am doing. Just bow to the Statue of Man.'

17

Azaazeel said: 'Lord, I will bow only to You, and not to a copy of You.'

18

Azaazeel's argument not to bow to the Statue of Man put Allah in a reflective mood.

19

Allah thought of Azaazeel's refusal to bow to the Statue of Man as a sign of Azaazeel's devotion.

20

Azaazeel perceived he was getting through to Allah.

21

To drill his unbowing point further Azaazeel said: 'Lord, has the Statue of Man become Your equal?'

22

Allah said: 'I have no equal.'

23

Azaazeel said: 'Lord, You expect me to bow to a creature I am superior to? I am older and stronger than this creature. You created me from fire and You created him from stinking earthly soil, and fire is more noble than earthly soil. You have endowed me with feathers and light and the crown of nobility. I was the chief guard of Your paradise. I am Your Caliph on earth and the General of Your Raqee soldier angels. I am the guardian of Your earthly heaven Birqi. I have worshipped You in paradise and on earth. I have...'

24
Allah cut in: 'Azaazeel! You dare question My Will?'

25
Azaazeel said: 'Lord, I am not questioning Your Will, but if
You spare me the indignity of bowing to Your new creature of
stinking earthly soil, I will worhip You more fervently than the
angels and with far greater zeal than before.'

26
Allah said: 'You will worship Me in the way I want, and not
in the way you want!'

27
Azaazeel said: 'Don't be angry with me, Lord. I can explain
everything if You give me a chance, O Magnanimous Lord of
Patience and Hope.'

28
Allah said: 'What is there to explain? You had your chance
like the rest of the angels.'

29
Azaazeel said: 'But I am not an angel. I am Your Azaazeel.'

30
Allah said: 'Then bow.'

31
Azaazeel said: 'Lord, how can Your Azaazeel bow to this
lowly creature?'

32
Allah said: ' I am Your Lord and Creator, and you do as I say.
Bow.'

33
Azaazeel said: 'Lord, I have a will of my own. Lord, You can

take away my life but not my will.'

34
Allah said: 'There is no other will but My Will. Bow.'

35
Azaazeel said: 'Lord, by forcing me and the angels to bow to this creature of stinking earthly soil You are dislocating Your hierarchical structure that sustains Your Worlds. If You think Your original hierarchical structure was misconceived straightening it up now will topsyturvy it again.'

36
Allah said: 'Everything I do is well conceived. For the last time, bow.'

37
Azaazeel said: 'Why should I?'

38
Allah said: 'Because I say so.'

39
Azaazeel said: 'Make me.'

40
Allah said: 'Bow! Bow! Bow!'

41
Azaazeel said: 'Slow down, Lord. No need to be snappy over nothing, O Lord of Patience and Hope.'

42
Allah said: 'You will bow! You will bow! You will bow!'

43
Azaazeel grinned.

44

Allah blasted: 'You are dismissed from your angelic position
as guardian of My earthly heaven Birqi, and you are no longer
My Caliph on earth nor the General of My Raqee soldier
angels, and you are banned from My paradise. From now on
you will be called Iblees, so you will never forget what you
have lost.'

45

Iblees was lost for words: 'But Lord...This is drastic Lord...
What I meant Lord... Please Lord...'

46

'Jibreel! Throw this Iblees of despair and gloom out of My
paradise! Now,' Allah screamed His orders at Jibreel.

47

Allah's screaming orders fearstung the bowing angels, and each
of the bowing angels said to himself: 'Thank Allah, it is Iblees
and not me.'

48

Armed with Divine Will and angelic zeal, Jibreel pounced on
Iblees, but Iblees eluded Jibreel's blow and escaped to the
Masjoor Sea.

49

But the sanctuary Iblees sought became his temporary prison,
for the Masjoor Sea angels apprehended him and ringed him
with their firespears and reported him to Jibreel.

50

Jibreel caught up with Iblees and, together with the Masjoor Sea
angels, chased him with stinging firespears out of the celestial
region of Dukhaan and out of the seven heavens and down to
the Euphrates in the first earth Adeem where Iblees disappeared
out of the sight of the pursuing angels.

51

The boldness of Iblees and the events that followed caused a commotion in the seven heavens which confused the paradisial and heavenly angels, and only the return of Jibreel and the Masjoor Sea angels allayed the apprehensions of the paradisial and heavenly angels who were assured that Iblees was out of the way and all was well.

SURA NINETEEN

The creation of Adam

1
Allah created the Soul of Man from His Own Breath four
thousand years before Adam.

2
The Soul of Man was different from the souls of the angels and
of all other creatures because the Soul of Man was bathed in
paradisial and heavenly lights.

3
When Allah decided to breathe life into the Statue of Man He
ordered the Soul: 'Get inside the Statue of Man who is in My
Own Image.'

4
But the Soul refused to go inside the Statue and said: 'Lord,
the mouth of the Statue of Man is deep and dark.'

5
Allah repeated the same order a second time and a third time,
but the Soul refused again and again to go inside the Statue.

6
The fourth time Allah just said: 'You will get inside the Statue
of Man whether you like it or not, and you will leave the Statue
of Man whether you like it or not.'

7
The Soul entered the Statue through its mouth and went to its
brains and stayed for two thousand years, then slid downwards
to its eyes, and when it reached its nose the Statue sneezed, and
the Soul tumbled down to the mouth, the tongue, the chest and
the ribs, and when it reached the Statue's bellybutton the Statue
looked at itself admiringly and said: 'What a beautiful sight,'

and then the Statue felt hungry and tried to move but could not move.

8
Allah observed: 'How impatient is this selfcentred creature.'

9
The Soul took another five hundred years to reach every part of the Statue, and the Statue became a living body with flesh and bones, blood, veins and muscles.

10
Allah covered the flesh of the living body with a translucent ungual membrane which grew more radiant every day.

11
Allah called the new Man creature Adam after the first earth Adeem.

12
Jibreel said to Adam: 'Adam, you are the first Man Allah has created in His Own Image with His Own Hands. Say thank you to Allah, Lord of All Creation, Who, in His Wisdom, created you out of earthly soil in His Own Image with His Own Hands.'

13
Adam said: 'Thank You, O Lord of Wisdom, Lord of All Creation.'

© Abdullah al-Udhari

Allah

1
Soldiers surprise Allah meditating in the Dome of
the Rock. Allah is stripped of His clothes, chased out
of the Holy Land.

2
In Beirut Allah is found trapped in the stunned
cries of a hundred and fifty million people. The militia
interrogate Allah, escort Him to the border.

3
Allah is caught stealing a loaf of bread in the
streets of Mecca. 'Shall we cut off His hand?' says
an officer. 'He's not one of us,' says another.

4
'We told you not to come back' blurts the president.
'That used to be my chair you're sitting on,' remarks
Allah.

5
Allah retreats to the Empty Quarter.

6
Oil is discovered in the Empty Quarter. Allah is exiled
from the Empty Quarter. Now Allah is a refugee in Baghdad
tending Arab children in His newlybuilt House Bait Ma'moor.*

© *Abdullah al-Udhari*

*The earthly Ka'ba of the angels

ABDULLAH AL-UDHARI

The silenced

SINCE World War II the history of the Arab world has been a catalogue of invasions, wars, civil wars, military coups, divine cleansing and bankrupt ideologies. The impact of this harassing turmoil led to the political and cultural break-up of the region and the disorientation and demoralisation of its people:

> Lord, our fear of the sun
> Runs in our blood. We have lost faith in light,
> We have lost faith in tomorrow
> Where we used to begin a new life.
>
> *Adonis: 'The New Noah'*

Modern Arab poetry has evolved against this tragically turbulent background. Poets tried to register the heartbeat of their times and voice the grievances and aspirations of their people and in consequence suffered all kinds of persecution. But since there was a spot on the map called Beirut where they could publish their work without the fear of censorship they were able to bear the strain of persecution. After the destruction of Beirut in 1982 by the combined efforts of the Arab and Israeli governments, the poets have been silenced for good:

Slit lips

I would have liked to tell you
The story of a nightingale that died.
I would have liked to tell you
The story...
Had they not slit my lips.

Samih al-Qasim

Now the national and political security services control all means of publication at home and abroad, and the poets have no option but to publish through them. By so doing the poets have lost their credibility and their work is no longer taken seriously. In the Arab world it is the integrity of the poet that matters and not his work. And this is the most devastating form of censorship.

The masses

They climb themselves, names indexed on windowless walls.

Abdullah al-Udhari

© *Abdullah al-Udhari*

ADONIS

Adonis (Ali Ahmad Sa'id) was born in 1930 in northern Syria and studied philosophy and literature at Damascus University. He joined the Syrian Social Nationalist Party in 1950 and was imprisoned for nine months in 1955, after which he moved to Beirut, where he was granted Lebanese citizenship. During the Lebanese civil war, he settled in Paris and in 1986 was appointed representative of the League of Arab States at UNESCO with Syrian diplomatic credentials. While in Paris he secretly joined the Syrian Writers' Union, which is run by the Syrian security service, though he was later expelled on the grounds of having read with an Israeli poet at an international conference. He now writes regularly for the Saudi daily Al-Hayat.

This is what Muhammad Ibn Isa al-Saidani wrote before he died

1
They have beaten me to another time,
They have entered the eyes of a dream, the body of light...
My body fights my body,
And longing
Urges me to leave to talk to my friends.

2
All these black dwarves are lost,
Only one shoulder,
The night is tired of carrying them.

3
'The roads have no outlets,
Houses and their days reduced to ashes,
It's useless to die now, nothing but loss.'

Don't block my sky

With your prayers.
Leave me to this beam I call my land.

4
Afraid...
Have I forgotten the road that once took me
To you?
Afraid... as if I'd forgotten its secrets,
        Forgotten our talk,
        Forgotten our words.

5
I see her grief
Like a dazed butterfly beating against the bulb.
I see her tearing her handkerchief.
I see my mother now,
        Her face a ditch, her hands
        Dried-up roses.

6
From time to time I feel as if I was someone else.
I feel as if I was blood flowing — I follow the flowing thread
        And ask: What is my name?
To think of what'll happen, I see myself holding my country —
        The fields, the mountains, the houses.
I say: To be sure I am,
        I have to die.

7
Comets falling from the terraces of space
I see them circling —
        I approach them and ask how they are,
        Greet their shadows
        And give them my body
        Wrapped in dust and cloth.

8
My body grows out of the grave
To build the sky as a home
With sunstrengthened walls.

9
He is a child of the sea,
His body is the depth of the sea,
His footmarks its open shores.

10
In his grave
He wore the face of a child.

11
He is dead, his hands
    Are like shadows on his cheeks.

12
We're going to him —
    A country beaming within wounds, our lamps.
Who said the winds threw us
    Over the walls?
The winds are our guides to him,
The winds are our keys.

13
Don't say I'm dead. Don't mourn me.
My death is just another shirt I wear.

14
Our villages
Are photo albums:
A photo of the tremor
A photo of the stars bowing at the doors of houses
A photo of lips dying
A photo of the moon
Taking off its shirt
To wrap it round the handsome victim.

© *Adonis*
© *Translation Abdullah al-Udhari*

SAMIH AL-QASIM

Samih al-Qasim was born in 1939 of a Druze family in Galilee. A Palestinian, he has been imprisoned many times for his political activities, but has refused either to leave Israel or to conform to authority. He is a prolific poet, believing that the 'only way I can assert my identity is by writing poetry'. He is a member of the Israeli Communist Party and editor of the Nazareth-based weekly tabloid Kul Al-Arab. He spurned PLO overtures to move to Beirut, maintaining that if people like him did not cling to their homeland, there would not be a Palestine.

The children…and my children

When children are born
They're given names
Chosen from the treasured family tree;
Their future secured
By saving schemes
And at Christmas
And other feasts
They're given new clothes.

When my children are born
They're greeted with affectionate tears
And the shiver of fear.
The eyes of mangy dogs
Are waiting for them
Police batons
And the longterm plans
Of the death squad
Are waiting for them.
When my children are born
Their tiny coffins are waiting for them.

© *Samih al-Qasim*
© *Translation Abdullah al-Udhari*

MAHMOUD DARWISH

Mahmoud Darwish was born in Palestine, near Acre, in 1942 but his family was forced to flee in 1948. Returning to Palestine but unable to return to his destroyed village, he felt like 'a refugee in my own country', a feeling reinforced by his imprisonment and house arrest by the Israelis. He joined the Israeli Communist Party, the only form of political representation open to a Palestinian, and was, by the late sixties, the leading poet of the Palestinian Resistance Movement. He moved to Beirut in 1971 but became increasingly disillusioned by the moral bankruptcy of the Palestinian leadership. After the PLO signed a peace treaty with Israel he returned to Palestine and edits the cultural journal Karmal.

In praise of the tall shadow

My country is a travel bag,
A travel bag is my country.
No platforms
No walls.

There's no land under my feet, so I can die the way I want.
There's no sky
Around me
To burrow into the tents of the prophets.

My back against a wall,
A fallen/wall.

My country is a travel bag
And my travel bag is a country of gypsies
A people living in tents of songs and smoke
A people looking for a place
In shrapnel and the rain.

My face against a flower,
A livecoal/flower.

My country is a travel bag
I spread out as a bed
And sleep on it,
Seduce girls on it,
Bury my friends in it
And die on it.

My hand against a star,
A star/tent.

My country is a travel bag
Made of the skin of my friends
And the nearby Andalus.
My country is on my shoulder,
Traces of my land in a foreign soul.

My heart against a rock,
A rock/freedom.

What do you want?
You're only a myth walking to another myth.
A flag?
What's the use of a flag...?
Can it shield a city from bombs?

How short is the journey
How large is the thought
How small is the state...

© *Mahmoud Darwish*
© *Translation Abdullah al-Udhari*

SHAMS LANGAROUDI

Shams Langaroudi (M T Javaheri Gilani) was born in 1951 in Langerod, a coastal city by the Caspian Sea. He has a diploma in mathematics and a degree in economics, and has worked as a teacher, journalist, cultural and economic specialist and editor. He has published five collections of poetry, a novel, a play and an anthology of Iranian poetry, as well as many articles. His most important research is his history of modern poetry in Iran in four volumes, which has been banned in Iran for years.

Pomegranate

You are no longer
the opened pomegranate
that is only remembered
by blood-coloured stains
on hands and mouths.

You are no longer
anything but a poem in the mouth
and the touch of your finger-tips
in our hands.

Astounding, ruby-coloured, polished, juicy
the opened pomegranate
will no longer remain on the tree

Requiem

I have come this long way
to see you.
I have seen the ploughed land.

I have seen broken mud–bricks
and the half–hidden moon.

I have seen children astonished
and grass trampled.

I have seen shadows cast by soil
and flames arising from sighs.

I have seen the wind
.............but not you.

© *Shams Langaroudi*
© *Translation Lotfali Khonji*

AHMAD SHAMLOO

Ahmad Shamloo, one of Iran's most respected poets, has been in trouble both before and after the 1979 revolution and has been arrested and forced into hiding or exiled more than once in his career. His collections include A Poem, That Is Life, *and* The Garden of Mirrors, *(Morvarid Publishers, Tehran, 1967), from which this poem is taken.*

Punishment

In this place there is a maze of prisons
and in each prison a myriad of dungeons
and in each dungeon countless cells
and in each cell scores of men in irons

One, amongst these men
Persuaded of his wife's infidelity
Plunged his dagger deep

Another, amongst these men,
Desperate to put bread in his children's mouths
Slaughtered, in the searing summer mid day heat

Some, amongst these men
On a deserted rainy day
Ambushed the money lender

Others, in the quiet of the alley
Crept stealthily onto roofs

Still others,
Plundered gold teeth from fresh graves
At midnight

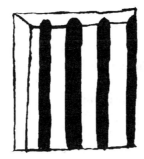

But I, I have never murdered on a dark and stormy night
But I, I have never ambushed a money lender
But I, I have never crept stealthily onto roofs

In this place there is a maze of prisons
And in each prison a myriad of dungeons
And in each dungeon countless cells
And in each cell scores of men in irons

Amongst these men in irons
Are those
Who can only come
With dead women

Amongst these men in irons
Are those
Who in their dreams see the final scream
Of the woman they have strangled

But I, I never seek anything in a woman
Unless — unexpectedly, serenely
She's there — my soulmate

But I, deep in my reveries, I
Don't lend an ear except to
The distant echo of a persistent strain

Of desert grass which
Sprouts
Shrivels
Withers
And scatters in the wind

But I, were I not a man in irons,
One dawn
Like a faraway, elusive memory
I would have transcended this cold, contemptible place

This
Is my crime

© *Ahmad Shamloo*
© *Translation by Ahmad Ebrahimi & Karina Zabihi*

VEDAT TÜRKALI

Notes for a 'bestseller' romantic novel

For Ünsal

So YOU think I can't write a love story because I'm too old? I'm absolutely determined to write one as if it had really happened.

First, I suppose, we need a pretty girl; that's not a serious problem. I have not just one, but several. Why do you look surprised? Wasn't it Karacaoğlan, our famous poet, who said, 'I fancied three beauties'? So it *is* possible! He complained that loving the eldest would be unfair to the youngest and he recited their names in turn, Şemsi, Kamer, Elif.[1] The poor poet of eastern Anatolia, where no birds fly or caravans move,...don't let him beguile you...by turning the rulers of night and day, and the first letter of Allah into innocent symbols over whom stretches a sheet of sky. It's he who says, 'If only I had a right to every beauty.' No need to find further evidence, it's clear what the crafty person wants. 'What kind of love is that?' you may ask, but don't ask, 'Can one write a novel about it?' Why not, if it finds a writer? It seems one beauty is not quite enough for such a lover.

This isn't our subject, let's cut a long story short. Let's drop the chatter and get down to the real business of telling our story. There's one problem: thousands of stories and novels have been invented about 'my one and only true love'; how do I know which one of the thousands you'd like? First, let's take stock and agree on one.

Don't expect any help from me — everyone to his own taste. But if you ask me, the most touching, heroic story ever told or written about 'my

one and only true love' is the story of Kerem and Aslı.[2] Kerem gets the
mother of his beloved Aslı to pull out all his teeth, one by one. He does
not utter a sound or care about the pain: he lays his head on Aslı's breast
and looks deep into her eyes.

You are right to think it unique; could any one of you pass such a trial
of pain or suffer so much for your beloved? Have you ever had such a
lover? Perhaps you'll call Kerem a fool; how could anyone take on such
pain if they hadn't been besotted by love? And can love which cannot
endure such suffering be called 'love'? Possibly, but it is not worthy of a
human being.

To cut a long story short, where shall I take you now? I'll transport you
to the plains of Bursa, the grass stripped bare, its trees removed and factory
chimneys belching out poison. In the past, when Bursa was mentioned,
our generation recalled the great Nazim[3] who lay for years in Bursa
prison, insisting always, 'How can the forces of evil come to light, if I don't
burn like Kerem, and you don't burn and he doesn't either?' Now Ismail
Beşikçi has taken Nazim's place in Bursa prison.

What is he guarding? The same as Nazim. Oh dear, my poor Turkey!
What a long duty this guard is!

We had received permits from the public prosecutor, and arrived at the
prison in the company of Ekrem, our good-hearted attorney. At the gate
they searched me right down to my socks. Thank heavens for those alert
guardians who perform their duties so well! This way, if an external
skulduggery penetrated within, both the state and the young men inside
would be punished. The prisons overflow with our young shoots of youth,
ensuring that our state and nation can come to no harm. We entered the
lawyer's office and Ismail, our Kerem, came and sat down opposite, with
his cheerful rosy face. We began to talk: our conversation was an endless
commiseration. Can Kerem be separated from his dedicated soul-mate?
They stripped the young publisher Ünsal of all his possessions and as
though that wasn't enough, they demanded money from him and planted
him in prison alongside Ismail. 'Either pay up or rot in prison!,' they said.
Where is Ünsal to find money when they had left him nothing? Any book
he published they declared harmful and removed, fearing it might sweep
away the dust from snoring sleepers and arouse the nation. It was worse
than the plundering of brigands! When the writers from all over the world
heard of this they united to rescue the dedicated man; 'This is a shameful
and disgusting business', they declared, 'let's save him, at least!' So they paid

up and he was released. One of our American women–writer friends saw the prison conditions: she came to Istanbul and held a meeting in which she reported how the prisons are full of our young. She wept as she spoke. As the saying goes, 'Even non-believers weep for our state of confusion!' and we also wept. But of those who wept together that day how many remained? So many returned to their own country. I'll return to this issue when we'll talk again about a certain 'somebody'.

Let us return to Ismail and what he said that day. He said what he always said; in short, 'UNLESS THE KURDS HAVE FREEDOM, WE SHALL HAVE NONE.'

Think hard; could there be a more direct, straightforward and intelligent comment than that?

'What's the situation now?' you'll ask. Here's how it is.

What can we do to get the dedicated publisher Ünsal for whose release from prison writers from all over paid bail, to once again publish the truth? Like the song torn from Kerem's heart. What's the right thing to do?

We should understand how Kerem met his end in flames.

First Kerem was wrapped tightly in the accursed magic shirt. 'We give you Aslıhan, take her', they had said, and placed Aslı and Kerem side by side. It was impossible to unfasten the magic robe: every time it was opened it closed again. As the sun rose, lovelorn Kerem uttered a sigh. A wild spark leapt from his heart and he died in Aslı's arms consumed in flames. And Aslı too burned away in his ashes.

That's how all those love-stories with unhappy endings finished; the Kerems and Aslıs in flames. How many young men and women have had their teeth and nails pulled out in agony and bloodshed, which explains why the prisons are overflowing. But who are the guilty? A question that must be answered, and while you are thinking about the guilty ones, Ünsal the publisher, is trying to find someone who can break the spell.

'Let's teach Aslı how to break the spell of that accursed black shirt; anyone wearing it must tear it off and cast it away,' he says.

Since the beginning of time, wasn't it the people who managed to break the black magic spells who were the best? We must let the people know about Aslı's story, so that their powers may be strengthened to the utmost.

We have come to the most delicate part of our story — in other words, if you haven't got rid of the black spell even Kerem's most passionate love isn't great enough to embrace Aslı.

This is *our* story — in the end we have no other love stories apart from the Kerems and Aslıs, the Ismails and Ünsals all burning: if you like, you can go around saying, 'If only I had a right to every beauty', but our own tragic love is devoted to one beauty only and to the loving heart that burns to death, crushed within the black shirt.

Let this be known, this is our perfect national love-story. You're welcome to it if you like it.

Let's come to a crucial point in our tale. How lucky for us that like Kerem-Ismail we are Turkish: Turkish like our dearest friend, the publisher Ünsal! When a Turk or a Kurd under any name lives in a country sharing in a heartfelt fervour, we too will sing songs of brotherhood with him and march along with him. Such folksong brings us to the subject of writer and publisher. If what we want is to save the people who choose the bitter pain of the black garments, the writer and publisher will plunge into that pain and find a way out together. Passionate love is a test: it doesn't admit lies. Kerem was no liar: lies are no part of the dedicated man. Let it be known that when the devil boils up his cauldrons of black tar, lies and deceptions are his fiercest fuel. Beware of providing the devil with fuel.

That's all there is to it. Coming back to that certain 'somebody', the story of this 'somebody' is a bit off colour. 'Who is guilty!' we asked. So now we'll dwell on this 'somebody' who could be a man or woman... There are a lot of 'somebodies' on earth. In our country a regiment of them march around. As regards a specially well-groomed company of writers/artists, anything that occurs to us about such a shameless crowd should be said without reservation.

If you call yourself human you love your country; if you call yourself a revolutionary you love your country; if you call yourself a patriot you love your country. Are there any who call themselves patriots who do *not* love their country? That is a bit complicated! Why did Eşper[4] keep yelling to his sister Sümru 'EVEN DOGS ARE PATRIOTS!' when he saw her smitten with love for Alexander who had attacked his country?

Would the great dramatist Hâmit lie? If what comes into your head when you hear of a dog's patriotism is a dog-collar and a heap of bones, is it Hâmit's fault? In other words he only wrote about what he saw around him. Since then wherever you look in our country you see a patriotic dog. There's a well-known traditional saying: 'A cur that doesn't snatch is like a horse that doesn't kick.' These curs certainly snatch: rushing headlong to grab the bones you throw them. When they hear the command, 'Fetch!', they grab even their own father, or yourself. So who throws bones to these curs, who holds the dog-collar? It's essential to know. In this commercialised world of ours it isn't easy to rear a cur with his baby-food, his vaccinations, his veterinary bills, his barber, his club but I don't talk of these... they are trivial. All you need to do is throw him a piece of poisonous meat, it vanishes immediately. You get used to thinking about trivia — but please — get used to thinking BIG!

The world you knew isn't the same any more; we know it is natural for the cur to leap at the bone — but now there are so many kinds of dogs, and an enormous number of bones that can't fit into anywhere! The second lot of 'somebodies' are those who are afraid of the big dog. He bites, you say, why not be afraid? But he bites whether you're afraid or not, and the more fearful you are, the worse he bites.

Don't let us forget that he has a street, a police-station, a truncheon, a law court, a mountain-top, 'jungle-laws', and the possibility of being the target of an unknown source. So be it. The fearful can come later: first you must collect the fearless, bring down roof and ceiling on their heads. There's no other way; the mill will keep turning unless you cut off the water. And what a mill! It's not wheat and barley the black millstones grind between them, but you and me. Did you realise who feeds these curs? If not, too bad. That's all from me. Suppose you couldn't cut off the water: it doesn't occur to you to cut off the miller. While you're thinking of the miller and the dogs, let us return to our novel.

The girl's called Dilan;[5] dark-eyed, dark eyebrows, hair down to her ankles, her forehead milk-white, cherry lips; she is tall as a cypress, graceful as a gazelle. She comes down from the mountain on her donkey, singing a plaintive song. Four or five curs waylay her, drag her beneath the rock. She weeps and pleads. 'Don't kill me. I'm promised in marriage.' They hold her feet and hands, and when she struggles they bring down a rock on her head and rape her. Shamelessly they steal her pretty shining garments, the blue bead round her neck, the mastic-gum from her mouth, even the donkey from beneath her. As you well know. Don't keep asking foolishly who they are. If you make me reveal their names you'll land me in more trouble. We have just rescued the publisher Ünsal from them. The tale I've told you has happened not once but a thousand times, and ever since the beginning of time Memo[6] has been on the mountain and doesn't come down. He talks of nothing but his Dilan's honour. He who knows, knows; if you are still unable to understand who they are, open your eyes and look around you closely. This is the work of all who stripped naked the Ayses and Fatmas, Ahmets and Mehmets; and what does it mean? It means that the day is near when those patriotic dogs who smile in our face and attack us will meet their end.

Memo will not come down from the mountain nor will men be brothers in our country until we are cleansed of the robbers and scoundrels and the pack of rabies-ridden curs. This is what you were born for — if you're a true patriot you'll say, 'aren't we the real owners of this land? You've played with our honour enough, we have suffered enough, they've done what they wanted to us, at least let's save our children.'

You have seen how our story leads to another, where it comes from, where it's going, how it exposed some filthy backsides in the course of its wanderings. In this country there are so many kinds of 'somebodies'! Now we'll start a new story: let's introduce ourselves. You've been listening to us all ears for half-an-hour. Whose side are you on? Are you one of them? Please clarify.

'How can you ask! Do you know who I am? I belong to the great INDUSTRIAL CORPORATION HOLDING for selling off the country...'

Evidently, you son of a bitch. Drop your loot and your Holding and come over here, you!

'Me?'

Yes, you!

'Your humble servant, sir, our consortium of banks and insurance companies — God be praised for them —'

I knew from the way you looked, you bastard! Leave your bank and insurance and get yourself over here!

'What will you do with me once you know about me? God gave me 10,000 hectares, along with my sons-in-law.'

Leave God's earth to God's hard-working subjects and come with your sons-in-law. Let's take you on; my good sir who can't bear to be separated from them.

Anyone left behind — let him come forward. Come on, why are you hiding? What are you waiting for, putting out the light and lurking behind the window like an Ottoman beauty waiting behind the blinds for her beloved who'll be passing her door?

There are no fields or factories or banks without your hands, your heads, your hearts. It's you who saved your country by making a rampart of your bodies. You said you saved it from the enemy. It seems there was something you forgot to do. Now finish the work before the country gets thrown to the wolves. Let's talk about the happy love-stories of Memo, who came down from the mountain singing, and doctor Aysun from Manisa, and Berivan the teacher from Hozat, and Oktay the computer-buff from Edirne. Let us write their stories. The earth will be adorned from end to end with love-songs and the fragrance of flowers. Enough of the smell of blood, it doesn't suit this beautiful land! ❏

This article is to be published in Turkey as one of a collection of articles whose royalties will go to Ünsal Öztürk, Ismail Beşikçi's publisher. Both men were imprisoned for their political views.

© *Vedat Türkali*
© *Translation Ruth Christie & Emre Azizleri*

Vedat Türkali *was born in 1919 as Abdülkadir Pirhasan. He was arrested on political grounds in 1951 and condemned to nine years' imprisonment, but was released in 1958. The following poem (which has now been set to music) was written in 1944 while he was serving a seven-year sentence for Communist activities and has since become a resistance anthem for all who struggle for greater freedom.*

[1] 'Şemsi', 'Kamer', 'Elif': Ottoman Turkish words denoting respectively: Sun, Moon, and the letter A.
[2] Kerem and Aslı: famous lovers in a Turkish folktale who suffer a tragic fate for their love.
[3] Nazim Hikmet: the best-known modern Turkish poet, who was imprisoned for many years for his beliefs. He wrote most of his poetry in prison. He eventually died in Russia (see page 55).
[4] 'Eşper', 'Alexander', and 'Sümru': 'Eşper' is the title of a tragic drama by Hamit, a late nineteenth century dramatist. Eşper's sister Sümru fell in love with Alexander the Great when he conquered their land and, accused by her brother of betraying her country, killed herself.
[5] 'Dilan': Kurdish woman's name.
[6] 'Memo': Kurdish diminutive for the most common name for a male, Mehmed.

Istanbul

*Dedicated to the memory of the poet of 'Fog'**

When the dawn winds blow in clusters
I think of you Istanbul from far away
Your ships that rend the blue canvas
Night in your Golden Horn of a thousand and one masts
Spring-tide in your islands
Sun on your Süleymaniye Mosque
Oh, city of our struggle, you are so comely!

And these days as I think of you from far away Istanbul
The darkness of your nights in my gaze
Your voice in my ears
And from far away
As I think of you from far away these days
You are now in the clutches of the forty thieves

On your beaches
Black marketeers have sprawled their greasy bodies on the sands
Virgins who've had abortions cavort before them
Together they harvest
The fruits of their fraudulent commerce in staple foods
You are now in the clutches of the forty thieves Istanbul

Meat butter sugar
Are the Sultan's three sons in your slums
Your children are raised on fables about eggs
There is no freedom
No bread
No justice
Your hands are chained behind you
Your roads blocked
No one save the forty thieves is entitled to live

A handful of profiteers contractors landowners
And their servile arse-licking friends
Their stringed instruments jazz villas doctors dentists
Have seized the reins
And you shopkeeper you peasant you state employee you intellectual
And you

You the worker from Ortaköy, from Cibali
Who talk of human rights
They kill you
They banish you
They pile their disasters on to your shoulders
To keep their silk mattresses lobster feasts and frivolous women safe
They condemn you to death

On a rainy March night
They rounded up the honest people who had spoken of human rights
In the dark dungeons of the city
A great day broke for the executioners
You have eyes that burn with the pain of your brothers
You have a pen-full of writings
A couple of words that scorch your mouth
Forbidden
The forty thieves have blocked the roads
The policeman's whip the hangman's noose
The speaker's mouth the printer's press
Are in the hands of the forty thieves
And the people
Conflict in their hearts victory in their hearts
The longing for children buried deep in their souls
Wait in their dungeons
Beloved comrades hide underground

We haven't endured all these agonies for nothing Istanbul
Behind the clouds there are drops of voices
Friends with smiling faces vested in courage
Have appeared before me
The pain in my temples has abated

I used to know a comrade
Wife of a brother
Emaciated bony shoulders carrying sick lungs
A sad face as she watched her babies
The day the forty thieves from their palaces
Ordered the executioners
In the ninth month of her pregnancy
In the middle of a stormy night
When hungry wolves attacked the suburbs
She brought on her back
From a far away village
Our secret of thirty-five kilos
Crimson victory gory victory

We haven't endured all these agonies for nothing Istanbul
Wait for us
Wait with your grand and serene Süleymaniye Mosque
With your parks bridges towers squares
Wait with your white-tabled cafes that lean against your blue seas
Wait for us
With your dirty children
Who sell toffee for a penny
And sleep huddled together in Tophane's dark alleyways
Wait for us to march through your streets singing songs of victory
Wait for history's dynamite
Wait for our fists to crush the empire of the forty thieves
Wait for those days to come Istanbul wait
You are worthy of us!

Akşehir, September 1944

© *Vedat Türkali*
© *Translation Moris Farhi*

*Tevfik Fikret

NAZIM HIKMET

Nazim Hikmet (1902-1963) escaped from Istanbul (then under Allied occupation) to Anatolia en route for Moscow in 1921. Between 1925, when he returned to Turkey and 1951, when he finally left it for the Soviet Union, he was in and out of jail for alleged Communist activity. Two of his major books, Poems to Piraye *and* From Four Jails, *were written in prison in the forties, and in his home country he was censored for many years. The sixties and seventies saw fuller publication but still possession of a Hikmet book was liable to get the reader into trouble. A biography is in preparation by Saime and Edward Timms. This poem is taken from* A Sad State of Freedom: selected poems of Nazim Hikmet, *translated by Richard McKane and Taner Baybars (Greville Press).*

Advice for someone going into prison

If instead of getting the rope
you're thrown inside
for not cutting off hope
from your world, your country, your people;
if you do a ten or fifteen year stretch,
aside from the time you have left
don't say:
'Better to have swung at the end of a rope like a flag.'

You must insist on living.
There may not be happiness
but it is your binding duty
to resist the enemy,
and live one extra day.

Inside, one part of you may live completely alone
like a stone at the bottom of a well.
But the other part of you
must so involve yourself

in the whirl of the world,
that you will shudder on the inside
when outside a leaf trembles on the ground forty days away.

Waiting for a letter inside,
singing melancholic songs,
staying awake all night, eyes glued on the ceiling,
is sweet but dangerous.

Look at your face from shave to shave,
forget how old you are,
protect yourself from lice, and from spring evenings,
and eat your bread to the very last crumb
and don't ever forget the freedom of laughter.

Who knows,
if the woman you love no longer loves you,
it's no small thing,
it's like snapping a green twig
to the man inside.
Inside it's bad to think of roses and gardens.
It's good to think of mountains and seas.

Read and write as much as humanly possible,
and I recommend you do weaving
and silver mirrors.

What I'm saying is that inside, ten years, or fifteen years
or even more can be got through,
they really can:
enough that you never let the precious stone
under your left breast grow dull.

1949

© *Estate of Nazim Hikmet*
© *Translation Richard McKane*

NEVZAT ÇELIK

Nevzat Çelik was adopted as a Prisoner of Conscience by Amnesty International after serving eight years for membership of a left-wing group, and was awarded the Rotterdam Poetry Prize for Persecuted Poets in 1987. An article in the Literary Review *which featured translations of his poems by Richard McKane, together with the publication of his poems in* Index, *contributed to the pressure for his release, as did the success in Turkey of his two books,* Dawn Song *and* Lifer's Song *(from which the poems printed here are taken) and prevailing political expediency. He started writing poetry in prison, following in the footsteps of his countryman, Nazim Hikmet, and writing with the same directness and simplicity.*

Pain's children

Pain's children — you burn brightly
the eyes of those who cannot look at you turn blind
like sheep who have lost their way
but in the bosom of the wolf there becomes a wolf

how quickly you grew
from whom did you learn to love like this?
tell me pain's children
how are you able to die with a smile on your lips?

pain's children the wolves that tear you limb from limb
are sick to death and lie in their lairs
everywhere the volcanoes erupt
your victory is in the death colour in your faces

January 1982

Dirty shirt

My hero may not be a hero
but don't hit me with those soulful songs
then my lines catch fire
each a burning star

star brothers we have one mother
a bare sword for the same love
we have undressed and we lie
in the night in the depths of prison

If I hadn't had my mother on my mind
I wouldn't have mentioned my pain
years mounted up after years I have not been able to kiss
my mother's hand so like mine

the silence descending with the nights
is an old wound opening beyond redemption
the walls have reared up again
be still my eyes defend yourself

if I strain out from my lines
pain death and the dampness of these walls
my mum is smelling my dirty shirt
smell my poem it's like hot bread

January-April 1982

Like a sun

Closing the tear
of your wound with your two hands,
you are carrying a star in your breast,
but that star will fall.

If you fall
one evening twilight,
you should fall like a sun,
and behind you thousands of shooting stars.

October 1982

© *Nevzat Çelik*
© *Translations Richard McKane*

AZIZ NESIN

Aziz Nesin (Mehmet Nusret) published his first volume of poems, Ten Minutes, *in 1957 at the age of 69, having been known previously mainly as a writer of humour, but later destroyed it. Most of the poems in it, including this one, were written in prison.*

Ten minutes

For ten minutes you sit,
your hands in mine,
the apple of my eye.
Ten times ten years not enough,
with prison guards to my right and left.
Prison's not so bad,
but this intensity of feeling is something else.
How are you?
I'm alright.
Where are those fine words of mine?
I long to take your face in my hands.
Autumn's the best season in Istanbul,
the perfect time for making love.
Clearly, they want to drive us mad.
But, fortunately we know the value of laughter.
I talk to myself now and again.
At night before the morning visit
as my eyes closed for sleep

I thought:
What can I give most sincerely,
Something from the heart?

I wrote this letter
these are the words I'm forbidden to speak,
by guards to the right and the left,
before me, behind me,
here, there and everywhere,
guards, guards, guards.
What thoughts I think,
but we must be silent.
In whatever needs to be done
commitment to the widest compassion
should be the only reason for merciless actions.
To establish endless peace must be the only reason for war.

These tears of ours,
our children will transform to lifelong laughter.
If we have a daughter, my love,
we should call her Gülsün[*]
don't you think?
Why can't they let people make love?
These hands, these eyes, these lips
are guardians of love.
Now more than ever before
I want to make people laugh.
But this love is different my darling
When morning arrives,
I'm filled with joy because you are coming.
I shave so carefully and comb my hair for you
It's all I can do.
I'll be seeing you for ten minutes.
I'll say how are you?
You will answer how about you?
Then we will be silent.
'Bye bye.'
As you go I'll be lost in myself.

A lock will turn.
Gates will close,
till next week's visit.
And I'll say to myself
Bring me the freedom in your eyes.

© *Aziz Nesin*
© *Translation Terry Tobias & Ruth Christie*

*A quite common feminine name in Turkey, from the verb *gülmek*, to smile or laugh. It means: may he/she/it smile.

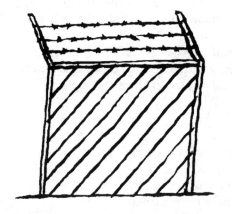

MEHMET YAŞIN

Mehmet Yaşin was born in 1958 and is a widely-read Cypriot writer. In the early 80s he wrote articles in Turkey condemning the policy of a separate Turkish state in Cyprus, which were suppressed. His first book of poems was condemned in 1985 for 'disloyalty to the motherland' and his second, published in Istanbul, was seized by the police and he was expelled as a 'foreign citizen'. He was imprisoned in 1987 when he returned to Turkey and is now settled in London.

Wartime

I was talking to myself so no-one could hear
my silence was read as wisdom!
Turkish was dangerous and must be hidden
and Greek was absolutely forbidden —
The grown-ups wishing to save me
waited each trigger ready like a machine-gun
anyway everyone then was a volunteer soldier.
English remained in the middle,
a slender paper-knife for cutting schoolbooks,
a tongue which must be spoken at certain times
especially with Greeks!
I was often unsure in which language to cry
the life I lived wasn't foreign, but one of translation;
my mother-tongue one thing, motherland another,
and I again completely different —
From those blackout days already it appeared
I could never be poet of one single land
being of the minority. And 'freedom' is
a little word uneasy in any nation's lexicon —
Finally in my poems three languages dodged about,
Turks could not hear my inner voice,
nor Greeks nor the Others —
How can I blame them, it was wartime!

© *Mehmet Yaşin*
© *Translation Ruth Christie*

RECEP MARAŞLI

Recep Maraşlı, now 41 years old, is one of the most eminent and scholarly activists for the Kurdish cause. He was first imprisoned at the age of 16 for his newspaper articles; he subsequently became publisher of the periodical Komal, *which focuses on the Turkish Kurdish community. In 1982 he was sentenced to 36 years' imprisonment, but was released in 1991 on condition that he did not 'reoffend'; he has since been rearrested. He is at present on trial for alleged membership of PRK-Rizgari, a pro-Kurdish group. These two poems are written in Turkish, though Maraşlı is Kurdish.*

You're not alone

Ignore
the fastidious romanticism of prison
forget sad poems
four walls
a bunk
your darling's wan face etc.

Look!
We're here
alive as 'the crazy spring outside'
clear as the blue sky
there's a bubbling life inside also

If one day my eyes cannot see
or if we part
never to meet again
I'll still be by your side

When you sing a song on your own
or get angry with people
or as you learn new things
I'll be in the sounds and the words

If you fall into darkness
I'll come
to your side with amazing lightless colours

When you roll in the emptinesses
or say the branch you grab breaks,
or a cell, an iron, oppression
don't ever say 'I am alone'
I'll be by your side

If you fall in love with someone one day
I will sense it immediately
I will be in your excitement
in your heart beats

If you make that big day without me
so many children's laughter
so many wizened old men
if you feast together with nature
Don't say 'If only he'd been here too'
I will definitely be there.

Diyarbakir prison, 1986

RECEP MARAŞLI

The hearing

The judge was judged.
A question was asked:
What's the crime?
'In death's sovereignty' the judge said
'living is the crime.'

The gendarme was handcuffed.
A question was asked:
'What is captivity?'
Obeying orders!

The jailer was locked up.
A question was asked:
'What is a cell?'
Man carrying the darkness within him.

THE SENTENCE WAS GIVEN:
THE SYSTEM HAS BEEN ARRESTED
HUMANITY HAS BEEN ACQUITTED OF ALL CRIMES

Winter 1991, Istanbul

© *Recep Maraşlı*
© *Translations Richard McKane*

KEMAL BURKAY

Kemal Burkay was born in 1937 in Turkish Kurdistan and studied law. He joined the Workers Party of Turkey (TIP) in 1965, and, after several periods of imprisonment, fled to the Federal Republic of Germany where, for two years, he worked for Kurdish workers and students abroad. He returned home in 1974 on the declaration of a general amnesty and was one of the founders of the Socialist Party of Turkish Kurdistan. He fled again in 1980 following the military coup, and has since lived in Sweden. He is the author of poems, short stories and novels; several of his poems have been set to music in Turkey and have enjoyed great popularity.

The journey

The humming of the days on the steppe
is sometimes like rain
perhaps the huge roses of the forests
are a flame within me
the cornfields pass by, the sunflowers, I'm travelling

Thinking back over the years, the partings
thinking back about a night on the Mediterranean
is it joy, is it grief
like the trains I carry it with me for years
the cornfields pass by, the sunflowers, I'm travelling

During a rainy spell your face blooms
it glows in the flood of sunlight
and I feel it in my very marrow
is it love, is it death
the cornfields pass by, the sunflowers, I'm travelling

The new day

In broken hope
in the clutch of grief
in pain, in poison, in the trap
don't despair
wait for the new day

For the new day
gives you a plum blossom
a Lake Van morning
a spark, a vibration
a clump of the Mediterranean Sea
a fresh coolness
and a young stretching
very tender rustle of hair
the new day
brings you
the gently damp warmth of a mouth
the melody settles like a kiss on your eyes
the cat touches your fingers like a lover
and battle and cruelty and fire
a song that all are working on together
to make it beautiful for themselves, to be beautiful
because life is a recurrent, twisting
burning silk thread
all of this
the new day
brings you

© Kemal Burkay
© Translations Komkar and Laimdota Mazzarins

In Praise of Free Speech

Borders Books and Music salutes Index on Censorship on the publication of **BANNED POETRY** and for leading the fight against censorship in all its forms around the world.

Borders is proud to join *Index* in hosting readings and discussions on banned poetry during Banned Books Week (September 20-28) at our stores across the United States.

We invite you to join us every day in support of international free speech and writers everywhere.

Participating stores:
Phoenix, Arizona · Los Angeles, California · Roseville, California · Torrance, California · Thousand Oaks, California · Washington, DC · Boca Raton, Florida · Coral Springs, Florida · Boise, Idaho · Champaign, Illinois · Evanston, Illinois · Orland Park, Illinois · Highland, Indiana · Wichita, Kansas · Boston, Massachusetts · Ann Arbor, Michigan · Birmingham, Michigan · Utica, Michigan · Bridgewater Township, New Jersey · White Plains, New York · World Trade Center, New York City · Fairlawn, Ohio · North Canton, Ohio · Tigard, Oregon · Springfield, Pennsylvania · Lewisville, Texas · Madison, Wisconsin

JACK MAPANJE

Leaving no traces of censure

I HAD always believed banishment from one's own country to be the most outrageous form of censorship that could be inflicted on any person; probably second only to execution. I had always expected it to happen to other people; I had spent my academic career trying to avoid it and had done nothing to deserve it, I thought. But six years ago my family and I were effectively banished from our country Malawi in southern Africa. This is what happened.

I had just been released from political detention at Mikuyu Maximum Detention Camp where I had spent three years seven months and 16 days without trial and without charge. During my imprisonment I had not been sacked from my post as lecturer in English at Chancellor College, University of Malawi. When police inspector general Lunguzi released me, he assured me that I would get my job back. Whoever doubted his dictate needed only to contact him; he would provide the Life President's 'official clearance', he declared.

When I reported my return from prison to university registrar Geoffrey Chipungu, however, he was dismayed by my presence. He wondered who had released me. He did not know what to do with me. He nervously appealed to university council chairman John Tembo who directed him to tell me to reapply for the job I had left in the university. I knew instantly that they did not want me back in the university.

These responses were predictable. I had heard that the global campaign for my liberation had bruised the Tembo-Kadzamira faction of successors to Hastings Banda's rule more permanently than it had damaged Hastings Banda himself. I had heard that the chairman of university council was enraged by my sudden release because he had not been informed beforehand. As one Special Branch person confided in me, Hastings Banda had detained me on the recommendation of John Tembo, his niece Cecilia Kadzamira, who is Banda's life companion, and his nephew David Kadzamira and Chancellor College principal.

I remembered my interrogation on 25 September 1987 when police inspector general Mbedza asked me, 'What have you done to each other in the university; you are not in our records; but His Excellency the Life President has directed me to arrest and detain you...' Inspector general Mbedza had boldly intimated that some university authority had reported me directly to the President.

I found John Tembo and David Kadzamira guilty because they were the only ones who had easy access to the Life President through Cecilia Kadzamira. And on my release on 10 May 1991 Hastings Banda's new police inspector general Lunguzi had declared: 'Only three people know that you are being released at this moment: His Excellency the Life President, me and yourself.' My extrapolation from this was to be confirmed by what was to follow.

I reapplied for my job. University registrar Chipungu took more than two months to acknowledge receipt of my letter. He replied in the third month after I had written a second letter in which I informed the university that I was going to the UK for a year's sabbatical leave with my family to recuperate from my prison experience and catch up on my linguistics career. In truth my relatives, friends, even strangers had urged me to seek greener pastures elsewhere before I was 'accidentalised' at the university where some of my friends and colleagues had died in mysterious accidents in the time I had been imprisoned.

Eventually we had to succumb and reluctantly leave. It was the most excruciating form of censorship we had experienced. We felt particularly humiliated to be offered protection from our own country by friendly foreigners first at home and then at Lilongwe International Airport from where we took British Airways.

AND yet Hastings Banda's 'henchpeople' such as university council chairman John Tembo, his nephew David Kadzamira, university registrar Geoffrey Chipungu, John Tembo's niece Cecilia Kadzamira and others, will argue that they never banished anyone into exile or prison, least of all us. And that's the point. Hastings Banda and his minions' 'eternal' censorship subtly left no traces by which the perpetrators could be pinned down in future. They let others perform their wicked jobs for them.

Perhaps the most outrageous legacy of censorship that our dictator and his sycophants invented for us is one where they censored without actually censoring; where they banned without invoking the banning order; where they censored us or our creativity by implication, by nuance, by suggestion; where they effectively let you ban yourself. Self-censorship is not an adequate concept to describe this kind of censure which was too subtle and too brutal for description.

One typical instance concerns my book of poems *Of Chameleons and Gods* which is believed to have been one of the many causes of my imprisonment. The book was never banned. The authorities contended that the book was merely 'withdrawn from public circulation'. When challenged about what this meant, the 'higher authorities' spewed out their explanation. Anything that is banned will be declared so in the government gazette, they maintained; it is therefore illegal to buy, sell, possess, loan, borrow, read or view the banned object. Anything that is withdrawn from circulation can be legally kept, bought, sold, loaned, borrowed, read or viewed.

No guarantees, no caveats were contained in their definitions and pronouncements regarding the consequences of keeping the object of withdrawal. That the object of censure was effectively not available for anyone to do any of the above because it had been withdrawn from circulation in the first place, did not form part of the argument. The paradox was that keeping the book on the shelf in one's living room was an offence which was neither culpable nor unculpable.

This type of censure is phenomenal; it throws the onus on the writer and not on the censor. You are meant to discover what it is you are supposed to have written to deserve the ban. You are supposed to feel guilty for having done whatever they claimed was subversive and this happened often when you had done no wrong, when there was no need for you to feel guilty. Malawi swarmed with informers who watched every twitch of potentially rebellious activity you made. When these saw the book which the censors had withdrawn from circulation on your shelf, they reported you or its existence to the 'higher authorities' and you were 'taken' into prison. The cyclic nature of their repulsive logic was remarkable and it always had calamitous repercussions on the victim.

The other form of censorship was embedded in the extra senses that the higher authorities ostensibly invested in ordinary words and expressions. You could not do anything substantive without getting 'official clearance' from the higher authorities. You could not perform a dance or a play or publish a poem, story or article without getting 'official clearance' from some authority first. You could not travel across country borders without a letter for the airport or border authorities to give you clearance to travel. No research in university or government departments could be conducted without clearance from His Excellency's National Research Council.

In reply to my letter in which I enquired whether my book had been banned or not, for instance, the incumbent chief censoring officer, Catherine Chimwenje, cautioned me for not having sent the manuscript of the book to the Censorship Board in Malawi for official clearance first before its publication by Heinemann Educational Books in London.

The next notion was that of the 'higher authorities' who were never clearly spelt out although upon probing they turned out to be an indiscriminate confusion of police chiefs, pioneer chiefs, army generals, principals of colleges, company managers, drivers, messengers, market vendors and other ordinary mortals. These loved hurling at you a multitude of expressions which were subtly meant to make you feel guilty for not conforming to the norm established by the dictator and his apparatus.

A banal expression such as 'biting the hand that feeds you' was often summoned when you even constructively disagreed with them. It was often used when they thought you were becoming too argumentative or too inventive for their liking. These expressions were invoked to shame you into submission.

Hastings Banda's world choked with institutions, notions, images, symbols and the language of control and censure. You were not supposed to be creative; you were not supposed to claim credit for what you had done; instead you were supposed to declare that if it had not been for His Excellency the Life President's wisdom, you would not have achieved whatever you had achieved.

If you did not achieve on their terms, the higher authorities looked at you or your achievement with suspicion, often embarrassing you into submission with massive claims that outside influence or collaboration with some exiles or dissident organisation or some western or Communist imperialist was involved. In Banda's Malawi it was dangerous to achieve anything on your own terms. And you were to be careful that the credit which you gave them was for your achievement only and not for your failure.

Hardly anything was done in your name, the country's name or in the name of the institution for which you worked. Nothing was done in the name of the people or in the name of humanity. If you insisted that whatever you had done was done on your own merit, you still needed to draw in Hastings Banda's wisdom and claim that without him whatever you had done would not have been possible. This way you were free from the charge of insubordination; free from detention; free from censure.

A ND yet these higher authorities and guardians of the nation's ethics were ordinary mortals. Their appointment almost reflected Hastings Banda's own amoral background. One Censorship Board chairman was a priest who had been discredited by the Catholic Church for apparently taking promiscuous liberties with his followers.

Another officer was a divorcee who blatantly claimed authoritative access to the incumbent secretary to the President and cabinet and head of the civil service John Ngwiri and had the special responsibility of watching over the potentially rebellious activities of the university.

The chairman and the chief censoring officer were assisted by a swarm of readers and informers some of whom were unambiguously illiterate. And yet the power which these 'higher authorities' brandished was so enormous that no-one was safe. Sometimes even the censors themselves were sacked from their jobs when it suited Banda and other 'higher authorities'.

These ubiquitous censors and their informers were strengthened by Banda's intelligence structure. There was the Police Intelligence, the Malawi Army Intelligence and the Malawi Young Pioneer Intelligence, each with a conspicuous array of informers. These were supplemented by other bizarre structures of intelligence and self-censorship established by each higher authority. Furthermore, the line between censorship and intelligence was blurred as each censorship structure and each intelligence structure vied for direct and independent access to Banda, Tembo, Mama or whoever was waiting for Banda to die for them to rule Malawi. The idea was crystal clear even to the youngest youth: no one intelligence or censorship system was to know what the other was doing. And each system was meant to outshine the other before the dictator and his minions. Either way the victims of the system were the ordinary people.

BECAUSE almost everybody suffered some form of censorship or self-censorship in Banda's Malawi we were forced to find alternative strategies for survival; alternative metaphors for the expression of our feelings and ideas. Writing was only one form of therapy; most of us did not write to seek fame or readership; we wrote to survive spiritually and to keep our sanity.

Today we can disclose how we circumvented the dictator's censorship. In the university the commonest method used by the radical academics who travelled to conferences was to send the censors one acceptable version of their paper and keep the original for presentation at the conference. If you edited a magazine, you sent the censors a batch of the materials to be used in the issue. After it was cleared you slotted in a poem or two which had not been seen by the Censorship Board.

However, this method was flawed. For instance, Robin Graham a colleague in the Department of English was deported for editing the university's literary journal, *Odi*, because someone had alerted the censors about a piece which he had included in the final version of the journal but which had not been cleared beforehand. The meeting which Robin had with university council chairman John Tembo to try and resolve the matter earned him the deportation.

And the victims of Hastings Banda's censorship in the Department of English alone are worth naming. Landeg White was deported for being adviser to a radical student broadsheet called *Vanguard*. James Stewart, professor and head of the Department of English under whose headship the department and the Writers Group flourished, was deported without explanation. David Kerr and James Gibbs were known by the Censorship Board for their boundless quarrels about the Travelling Theatre they directed throughout the country and the controversial plays they put on at the university's Open Air Theatre or the Great Hall after battling for the plays' clearance. Kerr and Gibbs were not deported probably because they had learnt early the tricks of survival under the despot.

Then there were the department's local academics who, in effect, could not hurt a fly. Felix Mnthali, a fine poet, was inexplicably arrested one dawn and apparently charged with possession of classical records by composers from Communist Russia! Mupa Shumba employed a domestic worker who invented 'a letter from the rebels in exile' which was found under his pillow and for which he was arrested. Mnthali and Shumba were sent to prison for more than one year each.

It transpired afterwards that their detention had been motivated by the Banda-Tembo-Kadzamira larger design of cleansing the University of Malawi of academics and administrators from northern Malawi. The chief architect of this extreme form of censorship and 'tribal purging' was Banda's own Malawi Congress Party secretary general and administrative secretary Albert Muwalo supported by Special Branch chief Focus Gwede and Chancellor College registrar and Boston University political scientist Alex Kalindawalo. More than a dozen academics, largely from northern Malawi, were rounded up and detained for many years without charge, without trial and without explanation.

Perhaps the most horrendous case of the English Department's local victims of these extreme forms of censorship by Banda and his henchpersons was that of Blaise Machila whose academic career was cut short by my sudden arrest on 25 September 1987. Blaise had taken over as editor of the university's literary journal *Odi*. He too was having measureless controversies with the Censorship Board for defending contributions to *Odi*.

After my arrest Blaise stopped teaching. As neither my family nor my relatives and friends were told where I had been abducted to, Blaise courageously made it his mission to find out, travelling between the Eastern Division Police Headquarters in Zomba, the Southern Region Headquarters in Blantyre and the office of Chancellor College principal David Kadzamira, to find out the truth about my whereabouts.

For more than a year Blaise see-sawed between the two. Often he was tortured by the Special Branch on such occasions and dumped in stinking police cells crowded with criminals bleeding from police truncheons. Blaise continued to bother the principal and the police until the principal himself suggested to the Special Branch that they send him to Mikuyu Prison.

Blaise Machila walked into Mikuyu Prison one Saturday afternoon in handcuffs and leg-irons. Tears ran down our cheeks when we embraced. He was eventually released after two and a half years. In that time he had gone irretrievably mad. Hastings Banda's minions invented another explanation for this type of censure. 'Blaise was detained for his safety; for his own security; anything could have met him if he had not been detained!' they stated.

So, exile, deportation, murder and imprisonment shrouded in mysterious origins were the forms of censure which Hastings Banda's autocratic regime resorted to. The censors blacked out international news

on the radio, in newspapers, magazines and books. Banda's agents
blackened pictures, ripped out pages from books, magazines and
newspapers; they cut out sections of films; tore up or confiscated people's
clothes; they searched houses; censored anything and anybody. Malawi was
culturally subjugated. Soon the seven or so major cinemas in the cities of
Blantyre and Lilongwe closed. To date Malawi has no cinema. ❏

© *Jack Mapanje*

Jack Mapanje, *a poet and linguist, was imprisoned for three and a half years in
Malawi because of his poetry. He has published two volumes of poems,* Of
Chameleons and Gods *and* The Chattering Wagtails of Mikuyu Prison, *amd was recemtly Southern Arts writer-in-residence at the Open University, where
he completed his prison memoir and a third volume of poems. He is now an exile
from Malawi and is professorial research fellow at the University of Leeds*

The vipers who minute our twitches

'Son, venture into distant scrolling terrain
And marvel at God's umbilical cordage
Of peculiar hounds'; Uncle, this abrupt
Liberation, this dogged fear for our safety
From friend and foe is cause enough; may

These wavering village voices therefore,
These distressed handshakes of relatives
Who tremble to see us off hurt; when did
Our political dissenters ever get proper
Good-byes from their dearest ones here?

So, let the families of your kinsfolk dear,
Let these nephews and cousins mustered
In defiant solidarity make their hurried
Backhanded hugs before the informers
Gathered about register who was present

At these rebels' send-off, though what galls
Us now, if we are truly free, is whether ours
Are the last feet to abandon this beloved
Territory in disgrace for having lynched no-
one; is this the ban we so dearly dreaded?

May our British defender in light T-shirt
Shrewdly extend his welcome wink then,
May he walkie-talkie our delayed arrival
To his compeer upstairs: we'll feign smiles
In wonder, irritation and beholden shame!

And yet what spectacle my dear country,
What affront, what treason deserves this
Protection from you by kinder friends from
Far away? When did your warm heart go
Cold? And should we perhaps shake this

Tenacious dust off our blistered feet against
This beloved soil? What crime merits such
Covert parting on exit visas, exit air tickets?
And these children, these buoyant children
Where will they find the anchor to ride these

Breakers on their own terms? And this wife
So rebounding, this house of gentle friends,
What breach have these folks committed,
Uncle, which airport are we bound for, what
Story shall we claim we have landed to tell,

Which navels of alien hounds are we meant
To wonder at with our stubborn brood of folks
Left behind? And how long, Lord, will the vipers
Minute every twitch, laughter and tone of voice
Made by those sending off this rebel family?

Lilongwe International Airport, 17 August 1991

© *Jack Mapanje*

KEN SARO-WIWA

Ken Saro-Wiwa, Nigerian novelist, TV producer and poet and a strong believer in peaceful campaigning, founded the Movement for the Survival of the Ogoni People and was arrested on a charge of conspiracy to murder four Ogoni leaders; he had previously been charged with sedition. He was hanged on 10 November 1995 after a trial from which his lawyers withdrew in protest at the handling of his case. This poem is taken from his collection Songs in a Time of War *(Saros International Press, 1985).*

Corpses have grown

Corpses have grown
And covered the land
The xylophone of the deceased chief
Is still, has forgot the past.
Ancestral spirits driven from home
Walk tearful abroad
The orphaned land weeps.

We have squatted before the shrines
Have bled our knees in pain
The morning libation is vain
In vain the loud name-call
At the feast of new yam
The sacrificial cocks are dumb

The old year is dead
And the new, unheralded
By shouts of laughing children,
Seeps sadly into empty homes
And the mortar falls at dusk
In the empty bridal-chamber
Where lovers twined like snakes

Made soft music to silences.

Earth echoes with alien sounds
Stuttering rifles, weird moans —
And the harsh face of war
fills the land with abomination.

© *Estate of Ken Saro-Wiwa*

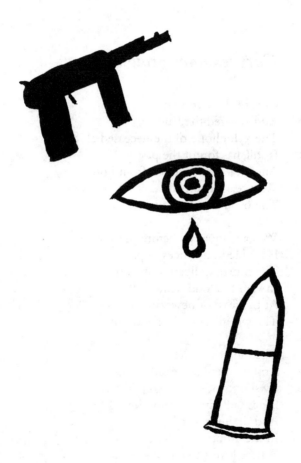

**Index *and* Waterstones
are proud to announce a series of
readings from the Banned Poetry
issue – taking place in branches
across the country on and around
National Poetry Day**

Thursday 2nd October
Waterstones Manchester
Michael Schmidt, Sophie Hannah, Jeffrey Wainwright

Wednesday 8th October
Banned Poetry reading, Waterstones Sheffield

Wednesday 8th October
Waterstones Islington
Peter Porter, Abdullah al-Udhari, Liu Hong Bin

Thursday 9th October
Banned Poetry reading, Waterstones Glasgow

MIN LU

Min Lu (Nyan Paw, 1934?-), the Burmese writer and poet, began writing at university and has published novels, poems and short stories. He was sentenced in September 1990 to seven years in jail for writing and (with the help of collaborators) distributing 'What has become of us?', one of the few examples of Burmese samizdat literature to have been produced in Burma since the May 1990 election. He was released in September 1992, but his colleagues are still in jail. The poem lists the actions of the SLORC since taking power, from the change in the name of the country to the army's massacre of students in 1988.

Quite unfair and cruel to boot

I have never heard
That a whole abdomen had to be opened up
Just to cure a mild case of diarrhoea.
I have never heard
That an entire pile of books was burnt
Just because a single termite blighted one.
I have never heard
That a spoilt child was stabbed
Just to scold him for crying for sweets.
I have never heard
That death sentences have been handed down
To minor violators of the Highway Code.
But I have heard that
The odious sentence of a lifetime's transportation
Has been given
For one small offence of rightly being angry
For just one day.

What has become of us? (excerpts)

PART ONE

What has become of us? They tell us we must
not pine for our aunt over mother's shoulder,
Yet they're telling us to hanker for our Chinese
comrades standing just behind father.
Their Air Force, their Water Force, their Fire
Force, or whatever...
Did I hear them say 'No-one but the military
Can gather up the country's earnings and keep them safe'?
I've heard the children chanting (they can't help it)
'S...L...O. R. C. Ha...Ha...Ha.Ha.Ha.'
What has become of us?
There are so many rumours nowadays.
They're telling us no-one died
On the steep levees of Inya Lake,
'They were just shot with rubber bullets'
'Just beaten with rubber truncheons'
'Only stabbed with rubber bayonets'.
Oh,...so this must be the Rubber Age
For all of us.

What has become of us?
Since they changed Burma to 'Myanmar'
Miss Burma became 'Miss Myanmar'
And the 'Do Bama Asi-ayone'[1] became the
'Do Myanma Asi-ayone'
Poor old Lord Mountbatten of Burma, he died
too early to be rechristened
'Lord Mountbatten of Myanmar'.
What has become of us?
In the auction of prison sentences
Where three years is the starting price
The man who said he wanted to see a glorious army
Hit the jackpot and won twenty years?[2]
No big deal.

Even the Shwedagon Pagoda
Has had to sign an undertaking to behave.

What has become of us?
You know that Text Law and Order
Restoration Council
Whose Chairman wears green glasses[3]
And his Deputy is Uncle Tom[4]
It's unbelievable!

And that man who dreams pink dreams in a red chamber[5]
While his fellow writers can't sleep from the bugs
on the floor
As he climbs the mountains of bones
And wades through the sea of blood
He'll get State money for his sentences
While the others get sentences for their statements.

PART TWO

'Look how we've resettled the homeless
With running water and lights which work.'
That's quite true. During the rainy season,
Their homes are full of running water
And in the hot weather the fires light the sky.
Or wasn't that what you meant?
Those trouser-wearers[6] who accused
Monks who were struggling for democracy
Of being mere 'yellow robe-wearers',
Can they really be the same people
Who try to bribe the monks with Lenten robes?

It's difficult to understand...
'We hate wars so much we have to fight them'
Are the words of an excellent storyteller.
I thought that I had heard that before
And now I remember where:
Surely they're the same words the American
President used to defend his Star Wars
project? Reagan's balls must have got stuck
In our man's mouth! As the press
correspondents already know
'As far as we're concerned
If you do thingummy, we'll do thingummy too,
If you don't do thingummy, we won't do
thingummy either, so we don't want you
to do thingummy.'
That was an ad hoc clarification brought to you
By the SLORC Information Committee.
That much is clear, isn't it?
That man, you know the one,
The one who shakes the hand of everyone
he sees ... Sec-One or something like it.
He points his finger here and there
But understanding nothing. So
When he points his finger, we're in trouble.
He's coming, he's coming!! The man they call
the Chairman of the State Parks and
Gardens Replantation Council.
His favourite pasttime: making speeches.
'I don't want to say this, but it has to be
said. What it is that must be said,
        I don't want to say.'
              It's quite remarkable!
'Our government is a legal government,
Our government is recognised by the world.'
That's right.
The world is as one in recognising our
government as the most shameless
in all the world.

PART THREE

Although they have abolished the one-party
system in Burma
We still live in a single-paper dictatorship
Where the *Working People's Daily*
Leaves a bitter taste in our mouths.

Some people say that
There is not a single true news item
In the *Working People's Daily*.
But it's really not that bad.
There is some news which is fifty per cent true
(I'm only talking about the weather forecast,
of course).

And once a month there is 100 per cent reliable information
(When they announce the lottery winners).

Hullo? What's that noise?
The sound of voices shouting their rallying cries
'Release all political prisoners now!!'
'Transfer power immediately!!'
Although the whole world can hear the shouts,
Are they just pretending that they cannot hear —
Or?[7]

'We are not bothered by
The threats of the big countries',
'And we don't care about the military tribunals.'
Oh no, of course not!
But they have already packed their bags
And searched for their boltholes,
While the younger ones
Will be left behind to die like pigs and dogs.
They'll be saying one thing now,
And another minutes later
'Don't do this', 'Don't ask for that',
Issuing their ultimata,
Telling lies repeatedly in their endless
press conferences.

'Tell Ah-wa-ara
To watch his mouth
Or he could be prosecuted'
Oh what a powerful threat!

No matter what happens
Don't ever lose sight of our
Three Main Causes, which are:
1)	Stay clear of the SLORC and avoid
	all dealings with them;
2)	Show solidarity with the students
	and follow their example;

3)   May all the monkhood and the laity
   help and encourage us.[8]

Only then
Will the spirit of the Fighting Peacock[9]
Raise up our people of Burma.

To commemorate the second anniversary of 8 August 1988

© *Min Lu*
© *Translations VJB*

---

[1] 'The We-Burmese Association' was a Burmese nationalist movement which began in 1930 in Rangoon, comprised mainly of students who referred to each other as 'Thakin' (master), the term which the Burmese were expected to use when addressing the British.

[2] Maung Thawka

[3] A Burmese saying — because of his green glasses he sees straw as grass.

[4] May be referring to writer Myint Kyaw, who translated *Uncle Tom's Cabin*.

[5] Mya Than Tint, a former left-wing writer who was imprisoned on Cocos Islands in the 1960s and 1970s, translated the Chinese novel *Dreams in a Red Chamber* into Burmese. He did not take an active role in 1988, and Min Lu may be criticising him for sitting back.

[6] A common term for army officers.

[7] Poet's footnote: 'People who hear the sound of poor people crying but close their ears and pretend not to hear, will not hear themselves crying.' (Hebrew saying)

[8] 'Our Three Main Causes' are SLORC slogans concerning 'Non-disintegration of the Union' and so on. The SLORC have hijacked the phrase *Doe Aye* — 'Our Cause' — and furthermore writers are now banned from using the spelling for our/we of *Doe* and must restrict themselves to the alternative *Toe*.

[9] Symbol of the Burmese Opposition movements and especially of students.

W S RENDRA

W S Rendra was born in central Java in 1935 and is one of Indonesia's foremost living poets and dramatists, and certainly one of the country's best. He started writing in the 1950s and 1960s and published his first collection of poems in 1957. Publication of 'Blues for Bonnie' (1971) followed an extended stay in the USA. Index *has recorded several of his readings being banned.*

Blues for Bonnie

Boston is withered and faded
from blustering winds, awful weather,
and a late night's bad luck.
In the cafe
an old black man
plays his guitar and sings
With barely an audience:
seven couples only
cheating and loving in the dark
billowing gray clouds of cigarette smoke,
like sputtering camp fires.

He sings.
His voice is deep.
He marries song and words
to give birth to a hundred meanings.
Georgia, far away Georgia.
Where stand negro shacks
with leaky roofs.
Earth worms and malnutrition.
Far away Georgia he calls it in his song.

People stop talking.
There is no sound
save that of the wind shaking window panes.
Georgia.
With his eyes clamped shut
the man hails silence
And silence replies
with a swift blow
to his gut.

In his perplexity
he acts the gorilla.
An old and stooped gorilla
roaring
his fierce fingers on the guitar
clawing
as he scratches the itch in his soul

Georgia.
No new customers arrive
The air outside is bitter
The wind blusters even more
And in the hotel
a cold bed waits.
The face of the cafe's proprietor sours
from the loss of an entire night
The black man looks upward
straining the cords in his neck

His eyes are dry and red
As he stares at heaven
And heaven
throws down a net
to snare his body within.

Like a black fish
he struggles in the net
Thrashing about
in vain
With anger
shame
and futility.

The wind beats across Boston Commons
Whistles in the church towers
and tears the night to shreds
The black man stamps his foot
as he sings his oaths and curses
His white teeth shine
in a tight grin of revenge
His face is dirty, wet and old
like a moss-covered stone.

Time, like a flood
overwhelms his weary soul
And in the middle of it all
he feels in his leg
a tremendous jerk.
Surprised
and near incredulous
he feels
the rheumatic cramp
rip through his limb.

In the performance tradition
he refrains from surprise,
and slowly stops

slowly rests on his stool
a cracked vase on a stand
in a secondhand store.
And only after drawing a deep breath
he begins to sing once more.

Georgia.
Far away Georgia he calls it in his song
His wife's still there
Devoted but suffering
Black kids play in the ditches
not at home in school
The old ones are drunks and braggarts
and ever and forever in debt.
On Sunday mornings they go to church
specially for negroes
where they sing
spellbound by the hope of the coming
and their absence of power on earth.

Georgia.
mud sticks to shoes
windowless shacks
Suffering and the world,
one as old as the other.
And heaven and hell
time-worn, too.
But Georgia?
Dear God,
Even after running so far,
Georgia is still on his heels.

© *W S Rendra*
© *Translation John H McGlynn, The Lontar Foundation, 1990*

LIU HONG BIN

Liu Hong Bin was born in Tsingtao, northern China, in 1962. After involvement in the events following Tiananmen in 1989 he went into exile and has since lived mainly in Britain apart from occasional visits to the USA and one return to China which led to a further expulsion. A student of English in his native land, he has continued to compose poems in his own language and has actively promoted contemporary Chinese literature in the West. Poetry has always been his chief love. He now lives in London.

Valediction

As I wait, illness makes me cherish every serenity
Words still squirm inside my throat

I will the words 'I love you' into her mouth
her breast risen, riverbank formed, my glances swimming

She spreads her legs and invites me in
I enter her to write
She says — when writing, to live is more important than to write
I say — when living, to write is more important than to live

Our children are being noisy in the next room
She: let them nip off a few of your poems
   let her know how to choose her clothes
   let him begin to think of how to think

Poets say that imagination is a kind of reality
one makes a home of a mirage when disaster calls

The past falls when it leaps up to the future
death could not forgive me for being a poet

I am the loneliness of a latticed window
Despair will not be anticipated by hope

Every day is the last day

Tonight I shall invite myself to attend my own funeral

Night is the silence of earth
bury me

Every moment is the last moment
Now I invite myself to be present at my own funeral

Night is the weightlessness of earth
entomb me

The willow tree unfastens its green hairbraid
night cascades like a lover's black hair
it caresses the bald heads of tombstones

At daybreak my bloodstream becomes a fire
burning, I am rainbow-hued and drained to nothing

Words are a gleaming river in the night
an elegy

All children who read poetry are my own dear children
their voices are like dawn breaking over darkness

Children I am back with you.

Standing at the doors of dusk

Standing at the doors of dusk
I open words
I see
darkness amid the silence
The world emerges
a man writes
with mutilated fingers
the square in his mind is empty

Bring your hands together
move to a safe place to pray
sprinkle water on silence
watch the voices of light expanding
now rip up that very silence

The doors of the world
unlock —
thousands of imprisoned lives
flee in the wind of dusk
I hear the banging doors

Instantly I shut the doors again
and find the pursuing words
have already been decreed

© *Liu Hong Bin*
© *Translations Liu Hong Bin & Peter Porter*

YANG LIAN

Yang Lian was born in 1955 and has been exiled from China since 1988. His work was first banned in 1983, but his efforts to build a memorial in New Zealand to the victims of the 1989 Tiananmen Massacre, and, more recently, a series of articles highly critical of the Chinese government have ensured that if he were to return to China, he would probably be jailed. He and his wife now hold New Zealand passports. His most recent works are Non-Person Singular *and the poetic sequence* Where the Sea Stands Still *(Wellsweep Press).*

Darknesses

1

green leaves always forgotten when   windows are too green
like every pebble roughly thrown by spring
hitting spring itself

birds   still wearing arid skates of blue
though old dog eyes are tired out

no need to translate the riverbank's slapping
the aesthetics of death   incite the swarming of the flowers

fields alone   can tolerate the furious heart
fleeing still further   April sniffs out blood
in sunlight the wood crouches behind us
knowledge that can't be taken away   it takes away the dead
reciting a poem   a deepened stillness

the other world is still this world   darkness would say

2
a storyless person   escapes into a day
with a gesture of escaping from the day

a pastless person   has passed away
seagulls worked into an abstract book by the evening

locked in the isolation ward   who isn't crazy
delusions   more like fragments than flesh

fragments of glass   shattering skeleton heard on the periphery
fragments of rotting tongue   twilight washes away, just washes away

rats squeal   shrill squeals as light stamps on itself
each day startled awake by each day

with one black night   a personless story
still won't come true told twice   darkness would say

3

each shower of rain makes you sit at your end
rain rapping on the roof   tiny animal steps
move you motionlessly into the darkness
in motionless weather you need others to sleep
to sleep is to leave   the world of the rainy season leaves
once darkness has passed through you like a thoroughbred through the fire
hear inside you   silvery white stitches everywhere
stitching a worn-out windcheater of flesh

every shower falls only on this bare ground
when you begin reading from your end   a page of black explanation
unweariedly swaps someone else for next day
forges an address   the graveyard street still muddier
finds fault with this hand   beggars huddle together in mutual hatred
making a city with nowhere to shelter from the rain
a flock of soaking crows collides inside you
breeds different crimes with identical faces   darkness would say

4

but darkness didn't say a thing   between dark and dark
only this spring

kite's bones hang in the treetops
bark shines   lovers pass kissing under the tree
pollen in the lungs beating last year's gong
a bright red clown   always makes children run wild

greener and greener the teeth that chew little hands
old newspaper lawn   hands over scissors of flame
so April   sees the river flow like a mirage
the current's forgotten colours   see us as mirages
once the dove's call is burned black   all the stars
are broken toys stuffed in a pitch-black floodgate

in darkness there's always a body drifting back to the place of no dreaming

even we fear   only fear our own terror
darkness doesn't say a thing   every walker on the streets
starts muttering to himself
darkness   is listening to the orange-red darkness of lipstick

a spring school always makes us ignorant
memory   who lives in it is a ghost
but sickness attenuates the look
when a mirror's worn on the face   the ocean digests a dead fish
being vomited is still endless chatter

darknesses are too many   for life ever to have got there
spring walks out of us   only then   is spring silent at last

© Yang Lian
© Translation Brian Holton

MIROSLAV HOLUB

Angels of extermination, angels of exclusion

S O MUCH depends on the red wheelbarrow, said Wallace Stevens. So much depends on every detail of the personal history.

In my experience, the censor of the Communist fifties was close to a hangman; the censor of the mid-sixties was a worried bureaucrat who wanted to live in peace with those 'above', but was easily infected by the ideas from those below. The censor of the seventies was just a mechanism to scare the publishers: an inadmissible literary work, usually the product of an inadmissible author, would simply not be permitted to be distributed, and this might cause the publisher's economic collapse. This was a very efficient kind of censorship which caused many of us to assume the noble status of non-persons.

For those of us who lived through the war and survived the fifties, the Prague Spring approached a freedom and enlightenment made by our own hands. For the younger generations it was just a pink Communism; it had to be rejected, together with most of the characteristic literary styles which could be described as kinds of critical or magical realism.

All views on the old and new censorships are strictly personal, depending on what we have personally experienced and known; with the reservation that we did not know many components of the cobweb in which we were embedded for most of our lives.

Recently, I was called to the Czech 'Office for Investigation and Documentation of Communist Crimes' and asked to report my complaints against the former totalitarian regime. I heard for the first time in my life that since 1969 I had been on the Black List which included several thousand people who would have been taken into custody or imprisoned in a camp if there had been any grave political unrest. I cannot now say what my attitude would have been if I had known that I was living in my own home on some sort of ticket of leave from a prison camp.

The emergency for which the Black List was drawn up never materialised. Between 1970 and 1982 I was just a non-person, checked twice a year by a policeman who would ask whether this was my house and that my car. There was no comparison between my situation and that of the dissidents who were imprisoned from time to time, or of the exiles who had the courage to abandon all those essentials we call home. But at least most of them were well informed about the cobwebs.

My attitudes to the different colours of censorship are influenced by my experience and by my conviction that the collapse of the totalitarian regime was brought about by the principles and good conscience of the dissidents and exiles, as well as by pressure from the so-called grey zone writers and intellectuals, and the bad conscience of some official, Communist intellectuals.

The dominant slogan after November 1989 was 'We are not like them.' My interpretation of this would have been that we should treat 'them', the Communist, official writers, according to their real literary values. Unfortunately, few of them had any real artistic merit (the good Communist writers became dissidents after 1969). Few of them were published in the new democratic media: so they became the new dissidents, bitter, aggressive, solipsistic; they developed their own literary ghetto in the new Communist press and they were joined, as were the true dissidents in Communist times, by some real 'anti-talents' who merely hated the new establishment. To hear their discussions with the present popular and published writers is a kind of sadomasochistic experience. The essential difference in their status is that they are allowed to live, albeit in the ghetto, whereas in the days when they had power, there was extermination.

There are other, major issues which restrict publication. First there is the economic control of the free market 'experts' who give priority to any 'comprehensible' idiocy, from occultism to medieval mysticism, because 'people want it'. They represent a new kind of Marxism-Leninism with a different colour.

Secondly, the new paradigm of 'real' literature which must be postmodern, relativistic, 'deep' (ie obscure), has produced a wave of intolerant criticism which disregards the vital link between what is being written and what can be read. The alienation of a broader public from the mainstream of present poetry is not the result of commercialism, but of an abdication by the poets themselves. The available space in the book market is filled by individual complaints on the state of the soul, the world and the nation; in magazines, intelligent, 'philosophical' speculations predominate over new literary contributions.

This, of course, is not a new wave of censorship, this is simply competition for the available space and time. The angel of extermination has been replaced by the angel of exclusion. This angel is not deadly, only boring.

It would be, however, very misleading to compare the angels of exclusion in most national literatures. In our situation in the Czech Republic, genuine and less conventional literature has less space, in book publishing and in magazines, than in a rich democracy. Compared to English literature, our writing shows much less continuity in style and human outlook, called also philosophy. This is due to the editorial policies and to the prevalent literary criticism which is readily reflected by all aspiring writers.

Basically, literature, and poetry in particular, are about human dignity. And we have human dignity now, even if we may not like the attitudes of our literary experts. Nothing comes under any heading of censorship any longer: only under the heading of 'communication' and 'solipsism'.

With the angels of extermination, one could lose one's life for 20 years or for eternity. With our angels of exclusion, we are merely wasting energy; the young ones are wasting their individuality. ❏

© *Miroslav Holub*

Miroslav Holub *was born in 1923 in Plzen and trained as an immunologist. After 14 volumes of poetry and five collections of essays, he still turns to science for some of his best metaphors for the human condition. His poetry combines 'a scientific gift for accurate observation with a poetic impulse to imagine'. His work has been widely translated, including his poetry collection,* The Vanishing Lung Syndrome *(1990), and a book of essays,* The Dimension of the Present Moment *(1990)*

OSIP MANDELSTAM

Osip Mandelstam (1891-1938) was not silenced until his famous 'Epigram to Stalin' (1933) led to his censorship, arrest and exile to Voronezh, where he was to write The Voronezh Notebooks *and the controversial 'Ode to Stalin', in an attempt to save his life and open the way to publication. Only his first three books,* Stone, Tristia *and* Poems *(1928) were published in his lifetime. The* Moscow Notebooks, *from which the poems printed here were taken, were written after a poetic silence of five years; 'Old Crimea' is based on his interrogation in the Lubianka. He was rearrested after the expiry of his exile and died of a heart attack on his way to one of Stalin's camps.*

Ariosto

Ariosto, the most pleasant, intelligent man in the whole of Italy
has gone a little hoarse.
He loves to name all the fish,
and pepper the seas with the most wicked absurdity.

Like a musician with ten cymbals
he leads the complex plot about knightly scandals
hither and thither, forever breaking
the music of narration.

He uses the language of the cicadas which is a fascinating mixture
of Pushkinian sadness and Mediterranean arrogance.
He is an incorrigible liar, playing tricks on Orlando,
and shudders and changes completely.

He says to the sea: 'Roar without thought!'
And to the maiden on the rock: 'Lie down without a covering...'
Tell us some more, we have too little of you,
while we have blood in our veins, and roaring in our ears...

Ferrara, you're a harsh town of lizards; there is no soul in you.
If only you would produce such men more often.
While we have blood in our veins
hurry and tell the story once more from the beginning.

It's cold in Europe and dark in Italy.
Power is as disgusting as the hands of a barber.
He plays the great man with increasing skill and cunning,
smiling from the open window,

at the lamb on the mountain, the monk on a donkey,
at the duke's soldiers, slightly simple-minded
with wine, and plague, and garlic,
and at the child dozing under a net of blue flies.

and I love his furious leisure,
his bitter-sweet stream of consciousness.
I'm afraid to pry out of the double-hinged shell
the pearl made of beautiful twin layers of sound.

Dear Ariosto, perhaps this age will pass —
and we'll blend your Mediterranean and our Black Sea
together into one brotherly blue expanse.
We've been there too, and we have drunk mead.

4-6 May 1933

'Old Crimea'

It's a cold spring. The Crimea is starving and fearful
and as guilty as it was under Vrangel and the White Guard.
The patched rags are in tatters, the sheepdogs are in the yard,
and the smoke is biting and pungent as ever.

The views are hazy, it is as beautiful as ever.
The trees are in bud, swelling slightly,
and are the real outsiders, and the almond,
blossoming with yesterday's foolishness, arouses pity.

Nature can't recognise her own face:
the refugees from the Kuban and the Ukraine are nightmare shadows.
The hungry villagers in their felt slippers
guard the storehouse gates, never touching the locks.

May 1933

© *Estate of Osip Mandelstam*
© *Translations Richard McKane*

BORIS SLUTSKY

Boris Slutsky (1919-1986), who lived in Moscow, was one of the outstanding Soviet poets of the twentieth century. He fought in World War II and was invalided out with a war pension. In the mid-sixties he broke finally with the official dogmas, saying, 'I have finished dancing your dances, I have finished bathing in your reservoirs.' Half of his work was still unpublished at the time of his death. 'I embellish reality' was written between 1959 and 1961 and first published in Novy Mir *1987 number 10. 'Those poems that I wrote and forgot' came out first in volume one of the three-volume collection published by* Khudozhestvennaya Literatura *in 1991.*

[Untitled]

Those poems that I wrote and forgot
and burnt before I could forget them —
there are not enough hammers and chisels
to knock them down and beat them down.

Those poems that I shouted out on the radio
and published in the newspaper:
better for me to have silenced them, so to speak —
I forged not steel but paper.

No matter! I'm still walking and breathing.
I'll still write something more revealing.

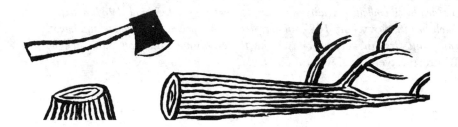

[Untitled]

I embellish reality —
I correct poems.
It's amazing to reread them —
they are both meek and quiet.
They're not only obedient
to all the laws of the land —
they conform to the norm!
They're true to the schedule.

They entrusted me to begin
the hunt after truth
so as they would be allowed
into print
through the back door.
So that the straight road
should lead them to the rouble
I break their arms,
I hack off their legs,
I betray utterly.

I embellish and lie...
Yet still I hide something,
still save something.
The most strong and gallant
I will not give up to anyone.

I will still publish
this book without corrections.

© *Estate of Boris Slutsky*
© *Translations Richard McKane*

LEONID ARANZON

Leonid Aranzon (1939-1970) was one of the greatest Russian love and nature poets. None of his poems were published in his lifetime; it was only in 1990 that a small book was published in Leningrad. His work was not political, so it is interesting to see poems of great fun, passion and exuberance being censored in the Soviet Union. Richard McKane's bilingual Death of a Butterfly: Poems of Leonid Aranzon *will be published by Gnosis Press in Moscow and Diamond Press 5, Berners Mansions, 34-36 Berners Streeet, London W1P 3DA*

[Untitled]

I live in those sorts of houses
which are empty, in which everything is terrifying,
and where one is impotent with fear,
where each door opens new phobias.
I love in them, and was loved,
and there was also a fear of losing love.

Any of Notre Dame's freaks
would be trivial in comparison, with, say,
a lady painted on the canvas
by someone out of medieval times,
then photographed for me
as a sign that the world lives by love.

I'm not talking about other utensils,
but every one could be a misery,
without any visible rival:
any thing has so many faces,
that one has to fall face down on the floor before it;
there is no measure in anything, everything is in secrecy.

I do not dare to trust emptiness
with its primordial, lying simplicity,
in it are so many souls, invisible to the eyes,
but one only has to glance to the side
and to see a few of them, or one of them,
instantaneously or later on.

And if even the eye is unable to see them
(bad sight, alas, is no excuse)
than it's obvious fear that will show those souls to you.
One is powerless to step over the line
that separates the world into light and darkness,
even light is a poor guard.

It's not death that's frightening me. I would not have wanted to live,
then what scares me in the dark?
Has my maturity still not conquered
my infantile alarm?
And I find terrifying what is ahead of me
and what appeared on the road behind me.

1966-1967

[Untitled]

I happened to see the sparkle,
the shining of the Divine eyes.
I know we are in heaven,
but that same heaven is in us.

It seems those who live unbelievingly
are not punished;
but no, each one is punished
by ignorance of the Divine shining.

I cannot prove who You are by example:
there is a shield between You and the world.
You can be proved only by faith:
the believer will see You.

I don't need Your favour:
not this life nor another —
forgive me, o Lord, the sin
of being depressed in Your world.

We are the people, we are Your targets,
and cannot escape Your blows.
I am afraid of one heavenly retribution:
that You will force the resurrection.

It makes me so alone to think
depressively as I look out of the window,
You are standing there too. A complete stranger
and in someone else's coat.

1969

[Untitled]

Horatio, Pylades, Altshuler, brother:
sister of mine, Ophelia, Juliet:
who, playing the masquerade for so many years,
is dressed as the gloomy Altshuler.

O, o, my Altshuler, I hope that with this
I too am Horatio, your Altshuler, Pylades,
and I am your sister, dressed up in the costume
of the composer of such a long sonnet.

Look here — here there is nothing at all!
My friend, my brother Ophelia, it's easy to make fun of you.
My neuter Horatio, you are living flattery to us all,

but don't be put out: I'm not joking with you —
where there is nothing at all, there is something else:
a sacred Nothing, which never diminishes.

May 1968

© *Estate of Leonid Aranzon*
© *Translations Richard McKane*

AGNES GERGELY

Agnes Gergely was born in eastern Hungary in 1933 (Hitler's year) and forced to leave school to work as a lathe operator in 1950, the worst year of the Stalinist trials. She completed her university studies in 1957 against the background of the final crushing of the Hungarian Revolution. For many years she was unable to publish, but is now the author of four novels and 10 collections of poetry.

Crazed man in concentration camp

All through the march, besides bag and blanket
he carried in his hands two packages of empty boxes,
and when the company halted for a couple of minutes
he laid the two packages of empty boxes neatly at each side,
being careful not to damage or break either of them,
the parcels were of
ornamental boxes
dovetailed by sizes each to each
and tied together with packing-cord,
the top box with a picture on it.
When the truck was about to start, the sergeant
shouted something in sergeant's language,
they sprang up suddenly,
and one of the boxes rolled down to the wheel,
the smallest one, the one with the picture:
'It's fallen,' he said and made to go after it,
but the truck moved off
and his companions held his hands
while his hands held the two packages of boxes
and his tears trailed down his jacket.
'It's fallen,' he said that evening in the queue —
and it meant nothing to him to be shot dead.

© Agnes Gergely
© Translation Edwin Morgan

JERZY JARNIEWICZ

Jerzy Jarniewicz (born 1958) is a Polish writer, critic and translator and the author of four books of poetry. He has translated British poetry for various literary periodicals and has contributed literary articles to Poetry Review, Agni, Irish Review *and* Literatura na Swiecie. *In 1994 he published a book of literary criticism,* The Uses of the Commonplace in Contemporary British Poetry: Larkin, Dunn, Raine. *This poem, written in 1978, was banned by the Communist censorship on the grounds that it gives 'a biased, defamatory account of the last 40 years of Polish history'.*

Short history

It was the Thirty Years War and
we went to ground under the debris
fearing
that we might be found by Wallenstein's mercenaries

When the Great Hunt was on
we kept hiding in the cellars
fearing
that we might be found by the blonde supermen
from Goethe's land

Today
we leave our rooms and walk the corridors
fearing that
nobody
will find us

© *Jerzy Jarniewicz*
© *Translation Jerzy Jarniewicz*

ZDZISLAW JASKULA

*Zdzilaw Jaskula (born 1951) is a Polish poet and director of the Nowy Theatre,
Łodz. He has produced four collections of poems, two of which were published in
samizdat editions. Translations of his poems have appeared in numerous
magazines and anthologies outside Poland. He has also translated the work of
Schiller, Nietzsche, Benn and Grass. In the 1970s, after he signed a protest
against the undemocratic changes in the Polish constitution, his works were
banned by the official media. His censored book,* Dwa poemaƚy, *1977, was one
of the first underground literary publications in Poland.*

My last will

If I was a son of a bitch, forgive
my mother who is not guilty of anything
Forgive my father if
I've proved to be an unworthy child of the regiment
I've been giving false evidence but absolve
the guilts of those who had to listen to me
Forgive policemen and mathematicians
for not counting my ribs
On my behalf say thank you to pop singers
and politicians for beautiful festivals
in the open air and in community centres
Tell them I've been effectively entertained
In writing express gratitude to workers
farmers and intelligentsia because machines didn't idle
the earth was giving fruit and minds
were mindful in all respects
Let those who didn't bid me good-bye
drop in tomorrow when I cool down a bit
Visit me anyway dear friends and
— if possible — buy me an alarm clock so
that at sunrise I wouldn't miss the light.

For instance

Someone said once, but
who it was I don't remember, that
each poem changes the world if only
by the mere fact that it exists.

It's a noble idea, yet I who am sitting
now at this (and not any other)
desk, in this (after all)
apartment, in this (well) city,
in this country (hard to believe) printing out some words (oh
words) on the typewriter
Predom Luznik 1301, not much
different from a sewing machine of the same brand,
I do not feel anything is changing.

I do not mean the things outside the window, the unchanging
'as long as we live',
the noises of children and TV sets, no. The skin,
what am I saying, bowels of the world despite my endeavours remain
     deeply
themselves. And I know that if I stopped
this poem at any moment, well,
here for instance

even then
nothing would happen.

© *Zdzislaw Jaskula*
© *Translation Jerzy Jarniewicz*

BOZOR SOBIR

Bozor Sobir, hailed by Khudonazarov as the greatest Tajik poet in 50 years, won the Rudaki Prize, the country's most eminent prize for poetry, in 1989. In March 1990 he was elected deputy in the Tajik parliament, but, disillusioned, resigned his seat in September 1991. In March 1993 he was arrested on a charge of inciting inter-ethnic hatred. He writes entirely in Tajik, a language itself interdicted in the Soviet era. This poem comes from a collection published in Russian in 1979.

The tree of poetry

Dedicated to Mumin Kanoat

It grows out of crumbling legends,
from slow wisdom, quick courage...

From flowing water, streaming moisture
neither life, nor escape for him —
it is sprinkled in living blood,
but only from the wound — from the heart of the poet.
The pain and alarm of red colour
for ever united with the ringing sound of foliage.

His spring shoot — a youthful prophet.
Our ancient language — his inner heart.
And each branch seething, as a vein,
under the mighty strain of impetuous lines.

Words — the weight of his life-giving branches —
they throw fruits at his feet,
better still — ripe fruits, by God blessed,
but how many unripe and bitter in taste!

There is a saying: for some distant sin,
from the almighty bows, arrows flew,
and touching the burning heart,
they would turn into a tree, soaring up,
towards celestial endless pride...

But to God — the godly; and the earthly — to the earth!
And the tree of the poetry I see
is an arrow, only not from the lifeless cold
— from the bow of all times, from the epochal quiver.

But for the shoot to break through the soil
doesn't the heart have to be touched
by the sharp edge of agony!
That your poem may rise
from the ashes of those who died for the just cause...

© *Bozor Sobir*
© *Translation Olga Ionova*

GORAN SIMIC

Goran Simic's collection of poems, Sprinting from the Graveyard, *translated by David Harsent, was published by Oxford University Press earlier this year. It is a fearless but lyrical evocation of life in Bosnia since the beginning of the war at the end of the eighties, centred on the siege of Sarajevo. Simic was born in Bosnia in 1952. He now lives in Canada.*

Sarajevo spring

It is spring again. The spring is coming.
It is coming in
on crutches. Swallows nest in the ruins.

Someone has strung a clothes-line
in the graveyard
and a hundred diapers semaphore the wind.

Peace surprised us: we needed more time
to pretend we deserved it, more time
to be 'the survivors',

as if we had plans, as if we knew
what next, as if
our dreams were not all of seagulls and the sea.

Peace is like a virus, a light fever.
Peace makes our Sunday suits
restless; it makes our shoes shuffle.

Soldiers wander the streets legless on slivovitz
asking, 'What next? What next?'
They won't go home

to collect their demob papers, they won't
hand in their uniforms;
well, what did you expect?

They needed more time, more time
like the boy we carried feet first from the movie-house,
wiped out by a happy ending;

like our neighbours, who've clean forgotten
how to keep a good row going;
like our local hero, a four-hundred-metre man,

who sits all day by the running track
in his wheelchair
as if it might suddenly come to him: what next.

Soon it will be medals and flags, a coat of whitewash
for the orphanage walls. The children carry
family albums with them

wherever they go. My friend carries
a child's winter glove. I think
he needs more time for this, more time, I think

peace has made us less than ourselves, and spring
is coming, hobble-
clop, hobble-clop, hobble-clop.

The story of Bešo

After a year in the Aussie cane-fields
Bešo had had enough: enough
of the smoke gun, enough
of the thick, black scribble
of snakes the smoke smoked-out, enough
of the cane-cutters who sold him
their daughters for shirt-buttons.

On the day he left, the manager
explained a thing or two: 'They thought
you had special powers. Do you remember
laying aside the serum and the syringe?
That was the day they took you
for their mulla-mullung, you see?
Their figure-flinger, their ju-ju man,
their little tin god. Know why?
Only such a man could cock a snook
at those five seconds of live-or-die
after the bite.' Bešo turned away
to hide the sudden panic in his eyes.

He moved on, taking up
as a poacher in the Northern Territory.
A Czech marksman would nail
the crocs, and they'd float downstream
where Bešo waited
to gaff them and haul them aboard.
Business was good until the police arrived.
That was the day Bešo found out
his pistol lacked a firing pin...
When they were free and clear, the Czech
explained a thing or two: 'My shots
were risks we *had* to take —
different with you; but, anyway, what kind
of chance d'you think a man would have

with a wounded crocodile?' Bešo lit up
a cigarette, shaking the match
to kill it, wanting to give
his shaking hands something to do.

Where next? Sarajevo — where else?
Back home... But it took a shell clear through
his apartment, front to back,
before Bešo decided to join
our colony in the cellar. 'Move it, Bešo!'
I yelled as I ran downstairs. He grinned
as if I'd cracked a joke,
grinned and stepped into the blood
of a neighbour whose body we'd shifted
only a moment before. I thought: Perhaps
he didn't notice the blood. Perhaps
he's got the idea it's just today —
just today, the shelling, just today
the stiff on the stairs. Perhaps
someone should explain a thing or two,
someone should tell him the war
has lasted a year. A whole year.
Has already lasted a year.

© *Goran Simic*
© *Translations David Harsent*

MICHAEL SCHMIDT

Homework: invisible censorship

CENSORSHIP first occurs when a writer revises and improves a text. This tolerable censorship is called 'revision': tracing authors through their drafts (if they have the courtesy or carelessness to leave them) can be illuminating. The next, still tolerable censorship is 'editing', when author and editor argue the toss.

Beyond these limits, moral and intellectual problems begin. Primitive censorship can start innocently at home. It is a short step from innocence to something more ambiguous, more tendentious: something that, if projected onto the big screen, would be matter central to the concerns of this magazine. Even so, at-home censorship is worth describing. Some advocates of free expression are not entirely innocent in their own drawing-rooms.

A writer withholds work from certain forms of publication. A poet who happens to be a woman might not wish her work to be represented in an anthology given over entirely to work by women, or in a feminist or radical-feminist anthology, even when she has a general sympathy with the cause the anthology illustrates. There have been notable cases of such withholding. One critic sees them as a failure of solidarity, another applauds the 'integrity' displayed. Other women writers won't appear in anthologies in which women's writing is under-represented. An Irish poet — even one born and raised in Ulster — may resent being included in an anthology with the word *British* in its title. A writer may resist having work included in a specifically gay anthology, since such inclusion is a form of 'outing' unless the poet is 'out' already, or politicises a poem or story in ways the author finds unsettling. Some writers whose work has been consistently misused prefer to withdraw it altogether, or insert a preemptive statement with it when it is anthologised. Some have felt that a major national anthology falsifies their culture and refuse to be associated with it. There is no compulsion to complicity on writers, and their insistence on the right to vet the contexts in which their work appears is unobjectionable in principle.

Another kind of withholding, less unobjectionable, begins in the firelit, brandied evenings of afterthought and repentance, provoked by critical hostility or by an author's own moral or ideological change. It starts, too, when the author wishes to protect work from critical 'misrepresentation', to guide the work's course through the journalistic and academic patristics that gather around it to direct and misdirect readers.

When a text is printed in a journal, it may still be subject to tweaking and adjustment. Once it has achieved the relative permanence of book publication, it has certain rights. And at that stage we as readers have certain rights also. We have a right of access, a right to read, to appraise and criticise. Once the text is in book form, the author has the same rights as we do, no fewer and (apart from the copyright income from anthology, quotation and reproduction fees) no more. A book or a poem in its integrity is part of the acknowledged record, whether the writer in the end likes it or not. The suppression of T S Eliot's *After Strange Gods* and of W H Auden's 'Spain 1937', of Borges's first two books, by their authors is a moral action which should properly be considered in this journal. They are attempts to change the record, to *unsay*.

Nietzsche refused to revise his early work later in life, on the grounds that the old man he had become would have been obnoxious to the young man he'd been, just as the young man, so full of dazzling, untested clarities, was obnoxious to him in his maturer years. Youth escaped the censorship of eld, and we can follow more or less certainly the trajectory of his work. Meddlesome people tried to adjust and censor the record posthumously, but Nietzsche's hands were clean. Pound's hands, too, are remarkably clean in this respect, which is why the contents of his work, the trajectory of his thoughts and prejudices, is so terrifying and illuminating. One might say the same of Gottfried Benn, Ernst Jünger and Hugh MacDiarmid, writers who do not seem to have tried to alter the record of their tragic intellectual growth. Milan Kundera has demonstrated how Kafka was distorted by Max Brod. But Kafka can be restored. Robert Lowell, on the other hand, couldn't leave his early work alone, so that the text of his poetry is destined to remain fluid for ever.

With the help of Auden, a crucial distinction can be drawn between proper and improper liberties. 'The Platonic Blow' is a poem which, printed piratically from time to time, is described as 'generally attributed to W H Auden'. If Auden wrote this piece of compelling homosexual pornography, he did not intend it for general consumption but for the amusement of close friends. A writer should have the liberty to write privately in this way. If the work escapes, it then belongs to the 'secret record', along with the letters and diaries and other bits and pieces which biographers stumble upon, and becomes (our good fortune) part of the 'parallel record', like Sylvia Plath's letters or Isherwood's diaries.

The case is different with 'Spain 1937'. Auden in middle life, repelled by certain phrases and by the cold delineation of its subject ('wicked doctrine', he called it), refused to allow it to be reprinted in the *Collected Shorter Poems*, though it had been one of his most celebrated pieces ever since its first appearance in 1937. He revised it substantially in 1939, even before Orwell's objections to it in *Inside the Whale*. But it still stuck in his moral craw. Revision could not make it palatable to the New Auden, who was by now rather old. Censorship was the course open to him: it gave the poem an enhanced celebrity, it cast a parodic light on the now carpet-slippered poet.

> We are left alone with our day, and the time is short, and
> > History to the defeated
> May say Alas but cannot help or pardon.

He deleted the lines in Cyril Connolly's copy of the poem in the 1950s, scribbling in the margin, 'This is a lie.' The poem has been restored to the record, and in *The English Auden* we have access to the 1937 and the 1939 versions. But for many years it was hard to get hold of, and critics were not permitted to quote from it.

Not permitted to quote from it. It is at this level that 'copyright censorship' is exercised, used invisibly and damagingly as a means of control. Of course a writer or a writer's estate should have the right to refuse quotation rights from unpublished work — letters, diaries, working drafts, and so on. A critic should have licensed access to the printed texts, and privileged access to unprinted materials. Yet as a publisher I cannot be alone in having signed agents' contracts which require me to let authors see the critical context of any quotations of their work that are applied for. I cannot be alone as an editor in having been asked to submit passages from essays to publishers for referral and correction.

One major press insists on these conditions usefully to correct misprints and bibliographical citations. Another will disagree with an essayist's emphasis or argument and refuse permission to quote. Another refers the passage to the author quoted, who then sends aggrieved letters to the publisher and the essayist, alleging treachery. In such cases the author or the author's agents are trying to fix the record. The kind of engagement where critic wrote and author replied, the clarifications that emerged from this dialogue, occur more rarely now.

If a writer has the right to withhold work from anthologies, why not acknowledge the right to withhold work from critical discussion as well? There is surely a difference in kind. The world abounds now in bad critical writing, it is true. True too that thousands of ill-prepared academics are trying to build young careers on the shoulders of established writers. Yet the real issue is one of free engagement with published texts. This freedom began to be eroded some 30 years ago, and the catalysts were not writers (it seems to me), but lawyers.

The process of erosion can probably be traced to American publishers whose legal departments, keen to avoid any possibility of breach of copyright suits, insisted that any citation in a critical context had to be licensed by the copyright holder. This overlooked the 'fair dealing' clause in the Copyright Act and meant that publishers were continually having to license critics to print short quotations from the writers on their lists. The cost of handling such applications meant that fees began to be charged on ever smaller tranches of quoted work. It meant too that those authors or agents whose contracts required the submission of anthology applications for approval could expect sight of the contexts intended for the three words or three lines to be quoted.

As soon as permission is sought for what ought to be covered by 'fair dealing', permission can be denied. The critic is no longer free to quote without the express approval of the person quoted, or of that person's agent or estate. The consequences for critical discussion are fundamental: in the end, there may only be the official, the authorised, the censored record. The horse's mouth will speak, and then the horse's mouth will authorise each agreeable interpretation of what it has said.

For the general reader and the academic, these behind-the-scenes tussles are almost invisible, witnessed formally on the acknowledgements page of the books they read. If the text has been adjusted to meet objections from a finnicky author, the reader is unlikely to know. If a chunk of an essay has been excised altogether because of caveats from an author's estate, the reader cannot find out. If I say that, three or four times a year, I am denied the right to quote from a writer in a book I am publishing, or that I have to deny a critic the right to quote from one of my authors because of instructions from the author, agent or estate, you may believe me or not. I cannot name names. If I could, those names would be familiar as individuals who would go to the stake for freedom of expression, whose voices have been raised in the public squares and the public prints.

At the heart of our insistence on free speech and free expression a double standard seems to exist. Perhaps it's as old as the cause itself, embodied in that first great monster of conscience, John Milton, to whose authority all those most voluble in celebrating our freedoms refer back. Robert Graves put it this way:

> By the time he had been made Secretary of State for the Foreign Tongues to the Council of State (a proto-Fascist institution) and incidentally Assistant Press Censor — why is this fact kept out of the text-books when so much stress is laid on the *Areopagitica*? — [Milton] had smudged his moral copybook so badly that he had even become a 'crony' of Marchmont Needham, the disreputable turncoat journalist.

Graves, notoriously, disliked Milton. Even so, it is worth considering this point.

It's the old problem of squaring private with public morality, taste and judgement with a proper respect for liberties. Before the publication of Philip Larkin's *Letters*, the editors at Faber wrote to the numerous people Larkin had maligned, asking their permission to allow the harsh things he'd said about them to stand in the published record. I received the request accompanied by the nasty passages they wanted me to approve. Having got on, I thought, rather well with the poet, I asked meekly whether he had not said anything less unpleasant about me. *No*, came the answer. I was tempted to refuse Larkin the right to libel me posthumously but in the end let his phrases stand. Later, I learned that many individuals had censored him, so that the harsh things he is permitted to say about those of us who respected his freedom to be unpleasant are all the harsher. Several of those who withheld consent are among the most voluble friends of the very freedoms they — in this instance — shied away from.

Sometimes censorship begins at home. Sometimes those who practise it are the very writers who most vigorously champion the freedoms they privately curtail. ❏

© *Michael Schmidt*

Michael Schmidt *is the editor of* PN Review, *editorial and managing director of Carcanet Press and senior lecturer in poetry at the University of Manchester. He is also a writer and anthologist. He is a fellow of the Royal Society of Literature*

ALLEN GINSBERG

Allen Ginsberg (1926-1997) was born in Newark, New Jersey and was early on associated with the Beat movement. His first collection, Howl and Other Poems, *was published in 1958; 'Howl' overcame censorship trials to become one of the best known and widely translated poems of the century. In 1965, within a few weeks, he was crowned Prague May King, expelled by the Czech police and placed on the FBI's Dangerous Security list. An edition of Ginsberg's poems, prepared in 1993 by the Polish publishers, Maszachaba, was ordered to be withdrawn and destroyed as a result of Catholic pressure. The following poems cannot be broadcast in the USA between 6am and 8pm, a relaxation by Supreme Court ruling of the Federal Communications Commission's original 24-hour a day ban, on the grounds of 'indecent language'.*

Imitation of K S

The young kid, horror buff, monster Commissar, ghoul connoisseur, attic bedroom postered with violet skulls, cigarette butts on the floor, thinks he'd strangle girls after orgasm — pumping iron 13 years old, 175-pound muscleman, his father shot at him, missed, hit the door, he saw his mother's tiny apron, father clutched his throat, six foot four drunk, today's in Alcohol Anonymous. Even eyes, symmetric face, aged twenty, acid-free-plastic packages of *Ghoul Ghosts, Monsters Nowhere, Evil Demons of the Dead, Frenzy Reanimator, Psycho Nightmare on Elm Street* stacked by his mattress; he followed me around, carried my harmonium box, protected me from the drunk Tibetan, came to my bed; head on his shoulder, I felt his naked heart, 'my Cock's half dead,' he thinks he'll cut it off, can't stand to be touched, never touches himself, iron legs, 'skinny dynamite,' thick biceps, a six-day black fuzz on his even jaw, shining eyes, 'I love you too.'

22 March 1987

I went to the movie of life

In the mud, in the night, in Mississippi Delta roads
outside Clarksdale I slogged along Lights flashed
under trees, my black companion motioned 'Here they are,
your company.' — Like giant rhinoceri with painted faces
splashed all over side and snout, headlights glaring in rain,
one after another buses rolled past us toward Book Hotel
Boarding House, up the hill, town ahead
                                        Accompanying me, two girls
pitched in the dark slush garbaged road, slipping in deep ruts
wheels'd left behind sucking at their high heels, staining granny
dresses sequined magic marked with astral signs, Head groupies
who knew the way to this Grateful Dead half-century heroes'
caravan pit stop for the night. I climbed mid-road, a toad
hopped before my foot, I shrank aside, unthinking'd kicked it off
with leather shoe, animal feet scurried back at my sight —
a little monster on his back bled red, nearby this prey a lizard
with large eyes retreated, and a rat curled tail and slithered
in mud wet to the dirt gutter, repelled. A long climb ahead, the girls'd
make it or not, I moved ahead, eager to rejoin old company.
Merry Pranksters with aged pride in peacock-feathered beds,
shining mylar mirror-paper walls, acid mothers with strobe-lit radios,
long-haired men, gaunt 60s' Diggers emerged from the night
to rest, bathe, cook spaghetti, nurse their kids,
smoke pipes and squat with Indian sages round charcoal
braziers in their cars; profound American dreamers,
I was in their company again after long years, byways
alone looking for lovers in bar street country towns
and sunlit cities, rain & shine, snow & spring-bud backyard
brick walls, ominous adventures behind the Iron Curtain.
Were we all grown old? I looked for my late boyfriends,
dancing to Electric Blues with their guns and smoke round jukebox walls
the smell of hash and country ham, old newspaper media stars
wandering room after room: Pentagon refugee Ellsberg, old dove
Dellinger bathing in an iron tub with a patch in his stomach wall
Abbie Hoffman explaining the natural strategy of city political saint

works, Quicksilver Messenger musicians, Berkeley orators
with half-grown children in their sox & dirty faces, alcohol
uncles who played chess & strummed banjos frayed by broken
                                        fingernails.
        Where's Ken Kesey, away tonite in another megalopolis hosting
hypnosis parties for Hell's Angels, maybe nail them down on stage
or radio, Neal must be tending his daughters in Los Gatos,
pacifying his wife, coming down amphetamines in his bedroom,
or downers to sleep this night away & wake for work
in the great Bay Carnival tented among smokestacks, railroad
tracks and freeways under box-house urban hills.
Young movie stars with grizzled beards passed thru bus corridors
looking for Dylan in the movie office, re-swaggering old roles,
recorded words now sung in Leningrad and Shanghai, their wives
in tortoise shell glasses & paisley shawls & towels tending
cauldrons bubbling with spaghetti sauce & racks of venison,
squirrel or lamb; ovens open with hot rhubarb pies —
Who should I love? Here one with leather hat, blond hair
strong body middle age, face frowned in awful thought,
beer in hand by the bathroom wall? That Digger boy I knew
with giant phallos, bald head studying medicine walked by,
preoccupied with anatomy homework, rolling a joint, his
thick fingers at his chest, eyes downcast on paper & tobacco.
One by one I checked out love companions, none whose beauty
stayed my heart, this place was tired of my adoration,
they knew my eyes too well. No-one I could find to give me
bed tonite and wake me grinning naked, with eggs scrambled
for breakfast ready, oatmeal, grits, or hot spicy sausages
at noon assembly when I opened my eyelids out of dream. I
wandered, walking room to room thru psychedelic buses
wanting to meet someone new, younger than this crowd of wily
wrinkled wanderers with their booze and families, Electronic
Arts & Crafts, woe lined brows of chemical genius music
producers, adventurous politicians, singing ladies & earthy paramours
playing rare parts in the final movie of a generation.
                                        The cameras
rolled and followed me, was I the central figure in this film?
I'd known most faces and guided the inevitable cameras room to room,

pausing at candle lit bus windows to view this ghostly caravan of gypsy
intellects passing thru USA, aged rock stars whispering by coal stoves,
public headline artists known from Rolling Stone & NY Times,
actors & actresses from Living Theater, gaunt-faced and eloquent
with lifted hands & bony fingers greeting me on my way
to the bus driver's wheel, tattered dirty gloves on Neal's seat
waiting his return from working the National Railroad, young kids
I'd taught saluting me wearily from worn couches as I passed
bus to bus, cameras moving behind me. What was my role?
I hardly knew these faded heroes, friendly strangers
so long on the road, I'd been out teaching in Boulder, Manhattan,
Budapest, London, Brooklyn so long, why follow me thru
these amazing Further bus party reunion corridors tonite?
or is this movie, or real, if I turn to face the camera I'd break
the scene, dissolve the plot illusion, or is't illusion
art, or just my life? Were cameras ever there, the picture
flowed so evenly before my eyes, how could a crew follow
me invisible still and smoothly noiseless bus to bus
from room to room along the caravan's painted labyrinth?
This wasn't cinema, and I no hero spokesman documenting friendship
scenes, only myself alone lost in bus cabins with familiar
strangers still looking for some sexual angel for mortal delights
no different from haunting St Mark's Boys Bar again solitary
in tie jacket and grey beard, wallet in my pocket full of
cash and cards, useless.   A glimmer of lights
in the curtained doorway before me! my heart leapt
forward to the Orgy Room, all youths! Lithe and
hairless, smooth skinned, white buttocks ankles, young men's
nippled chests lit behind the curtain, thighs entwined
in the male area, place I was looking for behind
my closed eyelids all this night — I pushed my hand
into the room, moving aside the curtain that shimmered
within bright with naked knees and shoulders pale
in candlelight — entered the pleasure chamber's empty door
glimmering silver shadows reflected on the silver curtained veil,
eyelids still dazzling as their adolescent limbs
intangible dissolved where I put my hand into a vacant room,

lay down on its dark floor to watch the lights of phantom arms
pulsing across closed eyelids conscious as I woke in bed
returned at dawn New York wood-slatted venetian blinds over
the windows on E 12th St in my white painted room

30 April 1987, 4.30-6.25am

© *Estate of Allen Ginsberg*

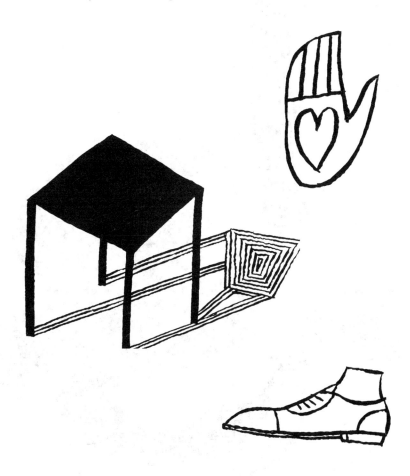

GORDON BROTHERSTON & LÚCIA SÁ

Poetry, oppression and censorship in Latin America

EVEN before Columbus set sail in 1492, oppression was denounced by poets in the part of the world now known as Latin America, as records in Nahuatl (Aztec), Maya, Quechua and other languages testify. Since that date, poets have continued to denounce while sometimes being silenced by the colonial regimes set up there by Spain and Portugal, and, from the nineteenth century onwards, by certain of the nation states which succeeded them. Salient cases are the military dictatorships which ravaged Brazil and the Southern Cone (Chile, Argentina, Uruguay) in the 1970s and 1980s, and which carried forward the spirit of the no less notorious yet cruder dictatorial regimes which had afflicted the Caribbean and Central America in earlier decades.

All along, the strong survival of indigenous cultures in the Andes and Mexico has complicated the usual modes of oppression and censorship. Indians in Mexico today talk of their languages as a means of articulating the world, concisely and poetically, according to pre- or non-western norms, and note the ever-larger threats posed to them by education in Spanish, political propaganda and the new commercialism. As the Nahuatl poet Luis Reyes says, referring to the constant threat posed by the *coyotes* or non-Indians in Mexico: 'Four hundred years have taught us/ what *coyote* wants' (see *Index* 1/1996). In the Quechua-speaking Andes, similar processes are lamented, and resisted, in the same terms, as is evident in sardonic native-language accounts of 'conversion' to Spanish in Ecuador. In Peru, Quechua has been the vehicle of songs and poems which contrive to incorporate Spanish words and habits of thought, in order to neutralise them politically.

At the same time, Mexico and the Andean republics have been chary of outright censorship. In Mexico, even the 1968 massacre of unarmed students in Tlatelolco has been written about in accusatory detail. José Emilio Pacheco's poem on the subject draws on Nahuatl accounts of Cortes's massacre of the local population in the same square in 1521.

In his great epic of the continent, *Canto general*, published half a century ago, the Chilean Pablo Neruda poured especial scorn on the dictators of the Caribbean and Central America, the 'traitors' who effectively sold their countries to US capitalists, silencing any objection in the most brutal and sadistic fashion. The Cuban poet Nicolás Guillén said the same thing in the collection he eloquently entitled, in English, *West Indies Ltd*. Exiled from his native Nicaragua, Ernesto Cardenal captured the absolute evil and absurdity of these regimes in his pithy 'Somoza unveils a statue to Somoza in the Somoza stadium':

> It's not that I believe the people erected this statue for me
> since I know better than you do that I commissioned it myself.
> Nor do I imagine it will ensure my posterity
> since I know the people will tear it down one day.
> Nor did I want to erect it while still alive
> as the monument that you will not erect to me once I'm dead:
> I erected it simply because I know your loathing of it.

In other poems, Cardenal draws directly on indigenous texts in the Nahuatl and Maya languages in order to place the plague of Central American dictatorships in the larger story of the oppression and homicidal silencing of voices that began with Columbus. In 'Katun 11 Ahau' he appeals to the rhetoric of the *katun* calendar cycle and the Maya books which had been destroyed in quantities by the European invaders: 'In this *katun*/ we weep for the burnt books/ for those exiled from the kingdom. The loss/ of the maize/ and our teachings of the universe.' Similar techniques have been used by the Salvadorean Manlio Argueta, author of censored novels and poems, who has had to spend most of his life in exile (see page 145).

As Neruda's epic again tells us, political resistance to the 'traitors' has often taken the very Latin American form of guerrilla warfare, which was born with Tupac Amaru and the Independence movements themselves. Guerrilla fighters, like Mao in China, were often poets, whose work necessarily reached the reading public by the most indirect routes. In cases like that of the Peruvian Javier Heraud, who was killed in action in 1963 at the age of 21, the poetry was very good indeed, beyond any question of political message (see page 152).

In both Cuba and Nicaragua, guerrilla resistance led to the triumph of a new social order, in which Guillén and Cardenal respectively played major offical roles, and where poetry was to be disseminated through state publishing houses.

As everyone knows, Fidel Castro's Cuba and Sandinista Nicaragua have been vehemently denounced in their turn as dictatorial and totalitarian. The true test case for Cuba was that of Heberto Padilla, who having lived abroad to escape the Batista dictatorship returned to collaborate with Castro in 1959, and spent several years as an official in Eastern Europe. Critics suggest that it was his experience of state socialism there, and the example of poets who had resisted it, which tipped the scales and led him to abjure the 'inspectors of heresies' at home. The shift was clear in *Fuera del juego* (1968; Offside), published by the state yet with a corrective preface by the Writers' Union; 'Poetica' sets the tone:

> Tell the truth.
> At least, tell your own truth.
> And afterwards
> accept whatever comes:
> they may tear your favourite page,
> they may shatter your door with stones,
> or people
> may crowd around your living body
> as if you were
> a prodigy or a corpse *(Translation J M Cohen)*

Padilla was harried and imprisoned and later left for the US, not before becoming a cause célèbre for Cuba's many enemies. There's no defending the treatment given to him, yet in the 'free world' its political significance has tended to be exaggerated, if only because Castro has been far less guilty of censorship and murder than many regimes over the globe openly supported by the US.

Under constant military attack from the US and its mercenaries, the Sandinistas in Nicaragua scarcely had the time or opportunity, during their term of power (1979-1989), to start discriminating systematically against poets they deemed politically incorrect. Their enemies chose rather to focus on their supposed hostility towards the culture and language of the Miskito Indians on the Atlantic coast. For the US in particular this represents quite remarkable hypocrisy, given that power's unswerving and massive support, at exactly the same period, for such genocidal regimes as that of Lucas García and Rios Montt in nearby Guatemala (under whom town after town of Maya speakers was obliterated), and given the Sandinistas' actually quite mild record in the matter.

Whatever the iniquities of Castro and the Sandinistas, they cannot be compared in any way with those of the dictatorships installed in the Southern Cone and Brazil, largely with the help and even direct participation of the US, in the 1960s and early 1970s. Kissinger's involvement with those determined to overthrow Salvador Allende's democratically elected government in Chile, often ignored in the western press, deserves to be proclaimed no less widely than similar behaviour in Angola, or his mass maiming of children and undermining of society in Cambodia. As Ariel Dorfman says, how can there be talk of reconciliation when the extent of the crime is not even generally known, still less conceded? The agony of millions of lives lost and ruined directly because of Pinochet and his fellow military dictators in Argentina and Uruguay is acutely caught in the poetry of Raúl Zurita, who witnessed some of the atrocity firsthand. From the Dantesque diction of 'Anteparaíso' (1982), Zurita moved to something far more intense and specific in 'Canto a su amor desaparecido' (1987; Song for the disappeared love), in what proved to be Pinochet's final days. In many respects an update of Neruda's 'General Song' of the Americas, Zurita's 'Song' manages to articulate the trauma of extreme torture and humiliation only by finding a correlative in the Native America, in the experience of peoples systematically silenced and dispossessed since the days of Columbus. Stanzas take the concrete form of tombs, each of 12 justified lines arranged six per page, which cry with pathos and anguish for the future of America (see page 146).

In the worst moments of the 1964-1978 military dictatorship in Brazil, censorship was vigorously enforced against the press, television, music, theatre and fiction. Not against poetry, however, which interested the censors less. Even so, poets like Ferreira Gullar and Thiago de Mello were driven into exile and their works circulated in Brazil only in small semi-clandestine editions. The economics of publishing poetry also worsened under the dictatorship, which led such 'Marginals' as Afonso Henriques Neto and Francisco Alvin to mimeograph their works and sell them in the streets.

By contrast, in the form of popular song, a key element in Latin American culture generally, poetry bore the full brunt of censorship during this period in Brazil. Chico Buarque had several of his songs completely banned while others were severely cut or changed. In '*Cálice*', composed jointly with Gilberto Gil, he addresses the subject directly through a pun between '*cálice*' (chalice or cup) and '*cale-se*' (shut up), in the biblical phrase 'father, take this *calice* from me'. The censors were not deceived however and prohibited the song from being played even without the words. Buarque's work is remarkable for seeking in colloquial speech a means of reflecting extreme forms of humiliation and abuse ('Say yes and you'll get on in life').

With Chico Buarque (see page 148), the censors seized on the subtlest political detail. In '*Tanto Mar*' (So much sea), the refrain *'pa'* — an interjection typical of Portugal — allowed the censors to identify, quite directly, a celebration of the end of the Salazar-Caetano dictatorship in that country, and the song was put on the index. At the same time, moral issues could be a problem so that lesbian references had to be eliminated from 'Bárbara', a song in the play *Calabar* which in its turn was banned at the last minute. Things got so bad for Chico Buarque that at one point any piece with his name on it was automatically banned. He responded by using pseudonyms (Julinho da Adelaide; Leonel Paiva), but these were soon exposed.

Chico Buarque was by no means the only one to suffer under the military censors in Brazil. When recording '*Escravos de Jó*' ('Job's Slaves') and '*Clube da Esquina*' ('Corner Club'), Milton Nascimento was obliged to leave out the words entirely. Geraldo Vandré was tortured so brutally that he could no longer write or perform. His '*Caminhando*', hugely successfully before it was banned, became a kind of touchstone and anthem for all those resisting the dictators. Caetano Veloso and Gilberto Gil ended up as exiles in London, where the former wrote and performed several songs in English, among them 'London, London' and 'It's a long way'.

All these poet-singers built up great solidarity with their counterparts in Spanish America, particularly the victims of the Southern Cone dictatorships; Violeta Parra who was silenced by Pinochet in Chile, and Victor Jara who was brutally murdered. The Argentinian Mercedes Sosa introduced songs by Chico Buarque and Milton Nascimento to Spanish America. A major factor in this alliance were the Nueva Trova musicians in Cuba — Silvio Rodríguez and Paco Milanés among others — who often invited the Brazilians to work with them. In the larger perspective, this indicates how strongly Latin American solidarity could be felt, in the harshest conditions, through shared song and poetry. ❏

© *Gordon Brotherston & Lúcia Sá*

Gordon Brotherston *is research professor at the University of Essex and full professor at Indiana University. He has lectured widely throughout the world. His recent publications include* Book of the Fourth World. Reading the Native Americas through their literatures *(Cambridge University Press, 1992; now published as* La América indígena en su literatura *by the Fondo de Cultura Económica, Mexico, 1997), and* Painted Books from Mexico *(British Museum Press, 1995)*

Lúcia Sá *is from São Paulo, Brazil. Her PhD dissertation was entitled* Reading the Rainforest: Indigenous Texts and their impact on Brazilian and Spanish American Literatures. *She has lectured on Brazilian and Spanish American literatures in Brazil and the United States and has published several articles in the same field*

MANLIO ARGUETA

Manlio Argueta was born in El Salvador, a state long known for the autocratic and violent rule of its '14 families' and the resistance this has provoked. Identified wiht the Universidad Centroamericana, Argueta established in 1987 the link between resistance and pre-Columbian roots in a novel, Cuzcatlan *(the ancient Nahuatl name of his country). Before the recent peace accords, his work was banned and he lived mostly in exile in Costa Rica. This poem was previously published in* Active in Airtime. A Magazine of Poetry and Prose *(Autumn 1992).*

Gentle homeland

My homeland is a hole ridden with holes.
A house of dead children. Men
and woman from here to there and from there to here, in tears.
       Flowers on the patio.
       Threatening friends.
You people that disappear in the war.

Gentle homeland. Ruined house.
Where jailors of hatred
make drawings with the points
of their silver pins.

Good morning sister bombardment.
Good morning human well-being.

Good morning sacred dead. My gentle homeland is like a bird.

© *Manlio Argueta*
© *Translation Chuck Wachtel*

RAÚL ZURITA

The Chilean poet Raúl Zurita, stayed to live through the worst years of the military dictatorship imposed by Pinochet in 1973. The horrendous, large-scale killings and 'disappearances' for which Pinochet was responsible are agonisingly reflected in Zurita's poetry, at first in an abstract Dantesque idiom designed to escape the censor, and then more directly in 'Canto a su amor desaparecido', 'Song to the disappeared love' (Editorial Universitaria Santiago, 1987). Four of the six-per page 'tombstone' epitaphs, together with the map of America in Zurita's 'Canto' are translated below.

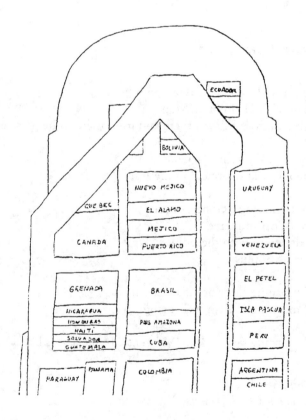

Camp 13: Passages and niche; placement is stated by countries according to dividing line

Song to the disappeared love (excerpts)

South American lands weeping. All taken by days, suffering and devouring lands in niches in Camp 13. From sands, Indian cities and worlds, they began the massacres and there was no pardon, amnesty or law. They died of hunger of love in dreams that are noted and named. They lie and rest in peace. At night their phosphorous glows and they emit laments. Source and complaint listed. Amen.

Araucanian niche. Placed in Camp 13. There were long valleys black like the other disappeared. It was reported so: southern planes furrowed the sky and then, bombing their own cities, shone for a second and fell. They are assigned to Camps with inscribed tomb and plaque. In quicklime they erased the remains and only the final wound was left. Amen. Everyone broke into tears. It was hard to contemplate. Amen.

Amazonia niche: from darkness and the play of shadows assigned to the Camp shown with corridor and site. All was hanging and cross with Peruvian and Brazilian lands. From the encounter the blood remains, the deserts of São Paulo and the Amazonia sky, it was said. It ws said to have been a river of blood and Paraguay. The blood still pulses its plaque. It says: stay and remain, Amen. No, it says the date. No, only Cross it says.

USA niche. Placed in Camp 12. Land of the north and designed to devour each other on account of dreams of space capsules, murders of blacks and hunger. Lower down were the sky and they were called Hiroshima in the lands that had food; lands of the Middle, Chilean valleys and devourers. All is night in the tomb they say in the American tomb. It lies like the buffalo in Peace. A Cheyenne phrase. It is written, Amen.

CHICO BUARQUE DE HOLANDA

Chico Buarque de Holanda was born in São Paulo and emerged in the 1960s as playwright, poet, song-writer and musician, though his plays were disrupted and his songs banned during the military dictatorship (1964-1978), and he spent a year in exile in Italy. He found ingenious ways of fooling the censors, the music alone suggesting the words of his songs. This poem was composed in 1972-1973 for the heavily satirical play, Calabar, *which was banned at the last moment.*

'Say yes and you'll get on in life'

if your body hurts
say yes
if they tighten the screw
say yes
if they sock you one
say yes
if they drive you mad
say yes
if they drool on your slip
give your cleavage a nip
give you a soft touch of the whip
hear me well

if they plaster you with mud
say yes
why make a fuss
say yes
if they tuck you up
say yes
if they bring you fame
say yes
if they call you mildred

stand on your head
if they leave you for dead
hear me well

if they shower you with gold
say yes
if they say you're through
say yes
if they suck up to you
say yes
if they curse your kin
say yes
if they fill your belly firm
with foetus and worm
no need to squirm
hear me well

© *Chico Buarque de Holanda*
© *Translation Gordon Brotherston and Lúcia Sá*

ANON

'Uyarilla' ('Listen') was recorded in Quechua (Quichua) during the grain harvest in Colta-Monhas, near Riobamba, in Ecuador in 1975, with the help of the local indigenous leader, Juan Remache. It illustrates well the conflict beteween the two languges and cultures of the Andean region, one inherited from the Inca, the other imported and dominant. Taken from Regina Harrison, Signs, Songs and Memory in the Andes. Translating Quechua Langage and Culture (University of Texas Press, 1989).

Listen

Uyarilla	Listen,
doña María	lady María.
maytagarilla	Where in the world
kambak wawaka?	is your child?
*iscuila*llamun	In grade school.
yaykukun ninka	He is enrolling, they say,
*colegio*llamun	in high school.
yaykukun ninka	He is enrolling, they say.
mana *valilla*	He's not worth anything
walindanguka	[his penis hanging down].
uksha chumbiwan	With a belt of straw
chumbillishkaka	he has kept his pants up.
*buena litra*ta	Good handwriting
japishpa ninka	he's got, they say.
*buena firma*ta	An impressive signature
japishpa ninka	he's got, they say.
*amu*kunawan	With all the big bosses
rimakun ninka	he is talking, they say.
*doctor*kunawan	With all the doctors
*parla*kun ninka	he is talking, they say.
*saluda*kpipish	When one says hello to him
manashi *parla*n	he doesn't speak.

*saluda*kpipish	When one says hello to him
manashi riman	he doesn't say anything.
*saluda*kpipish	When one says hello to him
mana chaskinka	he doesn't receive our hello.
*saluda*kpipish	When one says hello to him
mana rimanka	he doesn't speak.
alli *suerti*ta	A lot of good luck
charikushkaka	he has already held for himself.
*gobernadur*ta	From the governor
ña *gana*grinka	he begins to earn money.
chasna purina	Acting like that
layachu karka	he became a 'white.'
chasna kawsana	Living like that
layachu karka	he became a 'white.'
amukunata	From the *hacendados*
ña *gana*grinka	he begins to earn money.
jatunkunata	From the big bosses
ña *gana*grinka	he begins to earn money.
kunanka jatun	Now a great man
tiyarigrinka	he's getting to be.
kunanka jatun	Now a great man
tiyarigrinka	he's getting to be.
*deputadur*ka	As a political representative
*gana*gripanka	he begins to earn money.
alli *sueldo*ta	A good salary
*gana*gripanka	he begins to earn.

© *Translation Regina Harrison*

JAVIER HERAUD

Javier Heraud (1942-1963) was born in Lima and studied at the Universidad Católica, where he won a national poetry prize for his second book, El Viaje. *After visiting Moscow and Havana, he returned to join the guerrilla movement* Ejercito de Liberación Nacional. *He was shot by government security forces in the middle of the Madre de Dios river. His* Collected Poems *were published in 1964. This poem is taken from* Our Word. Guerrilla poems from Latin America, *translated by Edward Dorn and Gordon Brotherston, 1968.*

Poem

No,
I don't
laugh
at death.
It's just
that I'm
not afraid to die
among
birds
and trees

© *Javier Heraud*
© *Translation Gordon Brotherston*

ELISEO DIEGO

Eliseo Diego (1920-1994) was one of Cuba's most important twentieth century poets but is almost unknown outside Cuba, owing to the effects of the US-imposed sanctions which have served to isolate Cuba culturally as well as politically and economically. He pursued his career freely under the Batista dictatorship (when he co-edited Lezama Lima's literary magazine, Orígenes) and the Castro regime that succeeded it. His work is free of political or ideological prejudice; his themes are human concerns such as love, loss, fear, faith. This poem is taken from Los Días de tu Vida *(1993).*

Testament

Having arrived at a time when
The dusk no longer consoles me
And the smallest omens diminish me;

having arrived at such a time;

and as the dregs of the coffee
roundly reveal
their flat and bitter taste;

having arrived at such a time;

and lost all hope of
earning any preferment, of
seeing the sea untroubled by shadows;

and possessing nothing more than this time;

possessing nothing more, at last,
than my memory of nights with
its vast and vibrant delicacies;

possessing nothing more
between heaven and earth than
my memory, than this time;

I hereby make my will.
It is
this: I leave you all

time, all time.

© *Estate of Eliseo Diego*
© *Translation Adam Newey*

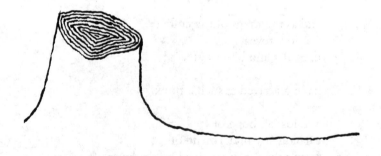

LAURA RUIZ MONTES

Laura Ruiz Montes was born in 1966 and lives in Matanzas. She is one of the young Cuban writers known as the generación inédita. *The name reflects the current state of the publishing industry which can no longer rely on huge state subsidies, but also the fact that many of them prefer to work outside the state structures, which further limits opportunities for publication. The following poem, written in 1993, was circulated in a handmade edition of 200 copies, and represents the writers's attempt to define herself in relation to the established poetic tradition as represented by Diego.*

To Eliseo Diego

I hail
this old man
who could have been so seductive
were it not for the fact that at times
he gets short of breath.
And so he parts his lips, breathes in,
and little by little
he sucks in all the afternoon
and me with it.
The city seems a home
made only for me to seek myself
in this man, who looks at me
from nearly half a century away,
as I imagine his hands.
I do not wish to see them,
I prefer to think that if they touched me
they would lay on my body an invisible thread.

Now we go sadly,
as if our desire
had sent us into absolute exile

and in some far place,
I had met a man so nearly seductive
who looked at me as if he knew me,
as if some other time
we had been lovers in a secret city
made only for me to be there
and for him to suck it all in
when at times he gets short of breath.

© *Laura Ruiz Montes*
© *Translation Adam Newey*

INDAMIRO RESTANO

Indamiro Restano, founder and vice-president of Armonía, a Catholic, non-violent Christian Democrat opposition group in Cuba, was sentenced in May 1992 to 10 years in prison for rebellion, disseminating counter-revolutionary propaganda and plotting to overthrow the government. No evidence was produced to support these charges. He also founded the Association of Independent Cuban Journalists (APIC). He was released in June 1995 but has since been forced into exile.

Inle

You learnt that the mystery of the sea
is worth more than language,
when they took you shyly
to the depths of the sands.
You were the love
that foundered on the sea and now begins to appear
riding on a huge cockerel.
The witches take
their spells from the cauldrons
and the sea opens
like a broken mirror;
because your fruits entered
the yellow animals...
Guide me in the silence of your love,
guide me, my love...

Clokun

Sailing through the sea I find you,
hidden in a froth
which the water distorts.
You raise yourself up
and the surface of the sea
blinds your body from times
which conjure the house of death.
It is the secret of the deep in its clarity,
which opens up holes in your eyes.
Song of the sea which has been waking
since the birth of the blue ants
which were sliding towards the earth
along the threads spun by spiders.
Spectre of knowledge,
which dances with the murderous fishes;
fountain of life,
transparent of stars.

Elegy

Nengro, I call you,
you guide me.
I blow away the mist,
you reply.
You open your floating eyes.
My centuries-old soul
groans its pain.
Your miracles are propelled
through the roof of the trees
and you run among the herds.
All that cuts me off from the future
is a star; bring it to me, Nengro,
to the shade of my cows.
I can hear the snail sing,
the mountain peak is bursting with clouds;
it is dreaming which takes me out of
my old gloom; give me back my dreams, Nengro,
in the heavy night.
The earth bellows, my bones bleed;
what takes away that huge tear
the size of distant alligators
is the water of the meadow
which dampens the grass;
take yourself away, centurion,
to that fountain of the moons.
Your frolics entertain me,
your wickedness hangs
from the tails of butterflies,
you become shy...
and you camouflage the pathways with their tigers
and they block the pathways with their birds.
Where are you, Nengro,
I call through the forest;
and you wander, a fugitive,
drunk on playing with the coconuts

Nengro, Nengro...
And my broken voice finds
your little guerrilla call
which imprisons the eternities
I breathe you in,
I give you sweets,
I snarl at you,
I tell you about the elephants;
I am like a bird delighting in the sun
when in the brutal silence
you bring your brightness.
But from time to time, a noise wakes me
I cannot see you
and with miraculous words
I exclaim:
Don't leave me, Nengro,
come, my Nengro, to bury all fear.

© *Indamiro Restano*
© *Translations Mandy Garner*

Index supports the UK premiere of

The Gambler

A story of
Love
and Money
based on an
incident in
the life of
Fyodor
Dostoyevsky

starring
MICHAEL GAMBON • JODHI MAY
POLLY WALKER • DOMINIC WEST
and TWO TIME ACADEMY AWARD WINNER LUISE RAINER

Directed by KAROLY MAKK

Produced by MARC VLESSING and CHARLES COHEN

Written by KATHARINE OGDEN, CHARLES COHEN and NICK DEAR

WEDNESDAY 29 OCTOBER

With introductions by Philip French, Film Critic of the Observer, and Karoly Makk

For tickets and further information please call Syra Morley at INDEX - 0171 278 2313

INDEX INDEX

MICHAEL FOLEY

The Princess and privacy

Had Princess Diana not died in a car crash in the early hours of 31 August while being pursued by photographers on motor cycles, and had one of them got a picture of her in the back seat of the vehicle with Dodi al-Fayed it would have been published on the following Monday. Instead we had the photographs of her former husband, Prince Charles, returning to England with her body.

It might, like so many photographs of her since she became public property — at least the property of the tabloids — have added to that sterile debate about the media and privacy that has been as quintessential a part of the British media landscape as the *Sun* and the *Mirror*. The ritualistic call for curbs on the press followed hot on the news of Diana's death.

Sections of the press itself have maintained that the self-regulatory system is working and that any alternative would be an interference with the right to press freedom. Newspaper owners will continue to take advantage of the lack of any real remedy for breach of privacy to publish whatever they like while simultaneously continuing to confuse people as to the difference between public interest and public prurience.

The right to privacy is a fundamental human right; as fundamental as freedom of expression. And that is where the debate should start. It is, like so many other debates about human rights, about balancing one right against another.

In Britain, the debate about media ethics and privacy has taken place purely as a reaction to the threat of government intervention. After World War II, the National Union of Journalists suggested some sort of regulatory system, but the proprietors would not play ball. In 1953, however, the Press Council was established with the co-operation of the proprietors because the government was threatening statutory control.

The Press Complaints Commission replaced the Council in 1991 but has been equally unsuccessful in preventing newspapers from publishing circulation boosting stories. In one famous case it condemned the publication of a photograph of Princess Diana sunbathing on a private beach while pregnant. The *Sun* showed its commitment to the self-regulatory process by publishing the offending picture again under the headline 'This is what the row's all about folks.' It also sold the pictures abroad.

Britain is almost unique in the EC in offering absolutely no protection to privacy. All other European countries have either a constitutional protection or have incorporated the European Convention of Human Rights into their law.

Had not Princess Diana died in Paris, changes were already on the way — even if the press had hardly noticed. The new Labour government has promised to incorporate the European Convention of Human Rights into British law and, with it, its strong statements on both privacy and freedom of expression.

Article 8 which states: 'Everybody has the right to respect for his private and family life, his home and his correspondence' will become part of British law, giving any citizen the right to go to court who believes their right to privacy has been undermined. The same European Convention recognises that rights have to be balanced; Article 10, which states: 'Everyone has the right to freedom of expression. This right shall include freedom to hold opinions and to receive and impart information and ideas without interference by public authority and regardless of frontiers', offers a protection of press freedom that is far more positive than anything currently in British law.

Geoffrey Robertson, QC, has argued in *Freedom, the Individual and the Law,* that its failure to protect the privacy of its citizens is the 'most glaring deficiency in English law'. That failure reflects the nature of a society both prurient and prudish 'where the newspapers which are the most despised for invading private lives are at the same time the most popular.'

Geoffrey Robertson argues that the press's freedom to serve the public interest would be 'better secured if privacy was protected by law rather than by systems which depend either on self-restraint (which is unworkable) or on extra-legal and unappealable power wielded by government quangos.' The USA, which has the freest media in the world, has developed privacy laws, fashioned out of Common Law.

The UK press should seek a deal with government: it will accept a statutory right to privacy, which it might have to do anyway under the European Convention; in return, government will reform the law of defamation, introduce a wide-ranging Freedom of Information Bill and abolish the Official Secrets Act. Again, the government might as well agree to this as the European Convention has been a remarkably effective instrument for achieving press freedom. ❏

Michael Foley *is media correspondent of the* Irish Times *in Dublin*

A censorship chronicle incorporating information from the American Association for the Advancement of Science Human Rights Action Network (AAA-SHRAN), Amnesty International (AI), Article 19 (A19), the BBC Monitoring Service Summary of World Broadcasts (SWB), the Committee to Protect Journalists (CPJ), the Canadian Committee to Protect Journalists (CCPJ), the Inter-American Press Association (IAPA), the International Federation of Journalists (IFJ/FIP), the International Federation of Newspaper Publishers (FIEJ), Human Rights Watch (HRW), the Media Institute of Southern Africa (MISA), the Network for the Defence of Independent Media in Africa (NDIMA), International PEN (PEN), Radio Free Europe/Radio Liberty (RFE/RL), Reporters Sans Frontières (RSF), the World Association of Community Broadcasters (AMARC), the World Organisation Against Torture (OMCT) and other sources

ALBANIA

Mujo Bucpapaj, a journalist with the newspaper *Rilindja Demokratike,* was shot and injured in Tirana on 20 August. Genc Pollo, a Democratic Party spokesman, said on 21 August that the 'ruling clique' was responsible, citing claims that Bucpapaj was shot at from a car with police number plates. According to Pollo, Bucpapaj had received anonymous telephone threats (*Index* 3/1997, 4/1997). Police said he had been caught in a gun battle between armed gangs. (RFE/RL, Reuters)

ALGERIA

On 26 June armed assailants killed Louisa Ait-Adda, a camerawoman with Algerian state television, in front of her house. Ait-Adda had suspected that a group of young people were planning to kill her, the local paper *Le Matin* reported. (RSF)

Abassi Madani, leader of the banned Islamic Salvation Front (FIS), has refused to comply with government orders to refrain from public comment and political activity following his release from jail on 15 July. After three days, during which Madani gave interviews to the press and met FIS colleagues, the interior ministry issued a gagging order. Madani was sentenced to 12 years' imprisonment in 1992. His release followed the freeing of Abdelkader Hachani, the third most important FIS leader. Hachani was sentenced on 7 July to five years in jail (time he had already served), for attempting to undermine state security, as well as three years' loss of civil rights. (*Middle East International,* Reuters)

Reports in late July suggested that Aziz Bouabdallah, who covers Algeria's Islamist groups for the daily *al-Alam al-Siyasi* under the name of Aziz Idris, has suffered torture during his detention. Since his abduction on 11 April (*Index* 3/1997), Bouabdallah has reportedly been held in Chateauneuf barracks. (CPJ)

Six journalists from the

French-language daily *al Watan* were given suspended sentences on 30 July for their roles in the publication of a report that had not been cleared by the official press agency (*Index* 4/1993). The article described an attack on a police station near Laghouat, in which five officers died. *Al Watan's* director, Omar Belhouchet, and reporter Nacera Benali received six-month suspended sentences; managing editor Abderrazzak Merad, and reporters Omar Berbiche, Tayeb Belghiche and Ahmed Ancer received four-month suspended sentences. Among the charges against the six was 'publishing false information that harms the security of the state and the unity of the country'. (CPJ)

ARGENTINA

On 23 June three men attacked the sister of Channel 13 reporter Antonio Fernandez Llorente in Buenos Aires, saying her brother had been 'talking too much'. Llorente has been investigating the January killing of photographer José Luis Cabezas (*Index* 2/1997, 3/1997) and alleges that businessman, Alfredo Yabran, is obstructing the investigation. Cabezas received many death threats prior to his murder. Other journalists who have been threatened in connection with the case are Ariel Garbarz, José Claudio Escribano and Magdalena Ruiz Guinazu. A .38 calibre bullet was placed on the doorstep of Guinazu's apartment on 2 July. (AI, CPJ, PEN)

Jorge Lanata (*Index* 9/1991, 2/1992), founder member of the Association for the Defence of Independent Journalism (Periodistas), was attacked on 12 July following his television reports on the privatisation of the state TV network, ATC, by its director, Horacio Frega. (Periodistas)

Two journalists, **Hernan Lopez Echague** (*Index* 4/1996, 8&9/1993) and **Dario Lopreite** received death threats on 13 July. Both are currently under police protection. (Periodistas)

AUSTRALIA

Recent publication: *Deaths in Custody: How Many More?* (AI, June 1997, 27pp)

AZERBAIJAN

Irena Lasota, editor of the quarterly *Uncaptive Minds* and president of the Washington-based Institute for Democracy in Eastern Europe, was searched by the military in Nakhchivan on 12 July, after she had interviewed former President Abulfaz Elchibey. Officers sought to confiscate any film, video or audio cassettes on which her interview had been recorded. Lasota's search coincides with a three-month campaign on state television against President Elchibey, chair of the Popular Front Party, who was elected for a term of five years in 1992, but deposed in a coup in 1993. (CPJ)

BAHRAIN

The interior ministry expelled German Press Agency (DPA)

correspondent **Ute Meinel** on 1 July for an article allegedly bringing discredit upon the royal family. Meinel was questioned for several hours about a report in which she quoted the London-based Bahrain Freedom Movement which accuses the royal family of threatening to bomb Shi'a villages. DPA editors defended Meinel, saying she had made it clear that the comments were made by the opposition group, not herself. (DPA)

BANGLADESH

Recent publication: *Institutional Failures Protect Alleged Rapists* (AI, July 1997, 9pp)

BELARUS

On 25 June the lower house of the parliament approved a draft press law in its first reading which will severely curtail freedom of the press if it becomes law in the autumn. The new legislation invests the State Press Committee with the power to close down media deemed disloyal to the government. (RFE/RL)

Stavislave Gusak, deputy chairman of the Belarusian Popular Front (BPF), and 14 members of the group's youth section, were detained on 27 July after a demonstration to celebrate the seventh anniversary of the nation's independence. Thousands of protesters gathered to chant anti-Lukashenko slogans and condemn his policy of closer integration with Russia. Belarus's official independence day was moved to 3 July by President Lukashenko

this year to coincide with Soviet expulsion of the Germans during World War II. On 8 August BPF member **Valentin Asta-shinsky** was fined after being found guilty of organising the unsanctioned march. (RFE/RL)

Journalist **Pavel Sheremet** and cameraman **Dmitry Zavadsky**, from the Russian public television station ORT, continue to be held by the Belarusian KGB in Grodno following their arrest on 22 July. They have been charged with twice illegally crossing the border with Lithuania, while filming a report on frontier security. The journalists could be sentenced to five years in prison, if found guilty. Sheremet, a Belarusian, has been a vocal critic of Lukashenko's government. In November 1996, the president threatened to expel him for 'lack of objectivity' and, on 7 July, he was stripped of his press accreditation after being accused of insulting the 'president and nation of Belarus'. Meanwhile 15 journalists from both local and foreign media were detained on 31 July for chanting 'Free Sheremet', while reporting the handing over of a petition for his release at the president's office. They were charged on 1 August with taking part in an 'unsanctioned demonstration' near a government building. Six were fined, and the others received warnings. (RFE/RL, SWB, RSF, *Financial Times*, *Guardian*)

On 15 August, a second ORT team was accused of violating

regulations while filming on the Lithuanian frontier. The four-man crew was fined and released, but detained again on the following day. **Anatoliy Adamchuk, Aleksandr Oganov, Valery Astashkin** and **Uladzimir Kostin** were held in Lida until their release on 22 August. On 18 August, President Lukashenko accused ORT of staging a deliberate provocation, but company spokesman, **Grigory Ratner**, claimed the crew was arrested to prevent discovery of a smuggling operation across Belarus's borders. Kostin was released from Lida on 25 August. (Interfax, RSF, SWB)

ORT journalist **Pavel Krashnikov** was stopped at Minsk airport on 17 August by police, who seized a video cassette and other material he was taking to Moscow. **Vladimir Fashenko**, another ORT reporter, was expelled from Belarus on 22 August following his detention on 18 August. Security officers forced him to leave the ORT bureau in Minsk to go to Grodno and give evidence in the Sheremet and Zavadsky case. (*Nezavisimaya Gazeta*, Reuters, RSF)

BOSNIA-HERCEGOVINA

On 3 July, the Banja Luka studios of Bosnian Serb radio and TV (SRT) were temporarily closed, following a dispute with President Biljana Plavsic. An announcer, broadcasting from the Pale studios near Sarajevo, said that staff were 'being subjected to pressure and blackmail to conduct their editorial policy, according to the *diktat* of the

office of the president of the republic.' (SWB)

SRT's director general, **Miroslav Toholj**, dismissed his deputy and Banja Luka studio manager, **Radomir Neskovic**, on 22 August for 'failure to comply with the editorial and managerial policy of SRT.' Two days later, the Banja Luka studio broke away and began broadcasting its own programmes, free from Pale's control. President Plavsic hailed the move as 'breaking the Pale stranglehold on state media'. SNRA, the Bosnian Serb news agency, branded it a 'media coup'. On 26 August, an attempt by 'unauthorised people' to take over the Duge Njive transmitter in central northern Bosnia was thwarted by police. (SWB)

BOTSWANA

The controversial Mass Media Communications Draft Bill was deferred on 3 July following a meeting between the government and a Botswana-led delegation of the Media Institute of Southern Africa (MISA). The bill had proposed the introduction of a newspaper registration system, a press council and the accreditation of foreign journalists. A task force, comprising officials and private media representatives, is expected to draft a fresh bill. (MISA)

BRAZIL

On 10 August government officials closed down the community radio station Radio Torre in the Butanta *barrio* of São Paulo and

confiscated its broadcasting equipment. **Davla Pereira** of Radio Torre said the station would take legal action to reclaim its equipment. (AMARC)

BULGARIA

Parliament approved a bill on 30 July permitting secret police files to be opened. The new law means the exposure to public scrutiny of all MPs, government officials and judges who may once have collaborated with the Communist intelligence services. On 8 August, the opposition Socialist Party, Alliance for National Salvation and the Bulgarian Business Bloc appealed to the Constitutional Court to block the law, saying it would jeopardise the normal functioning of the state. (Reuters, RFE/RL)

BURMA

Recent publication: *Ethnic Minority Rights Under Attack* (AI, July 1997, 22pp)

BURUNDI

On 31 July six people were condemned to death for their part in the recent ethnic killings, bringing the total of death sentences to 89 of the 150 cases so far examined. None of the accused had benefited from legal advice during their trials. (UN Department of Humanitarian Affairs, AI)

Recent publication: *Forced Relocation: New Patterns of Human Rights Abuses (AI, July 1997, 19pp)*

CAMBODIA

Recent publication: *Arrest and Execution of Political Opponents* (AI, July 1997, 9pp)

CAMEROON

David N'dachi Tagne, a Radio France International correspondent in Yaounde, was stripped of his accreditation on 7 July by Augustin Koundchou, minister in charge of communications. Koundchou accused him of wishing to 'tarnish the image of Cameroon', distorting the facts, and a 'clear intent' to create problems of law and order. He made no reference to any specific report by Tagne. (NDIMA)

Copies of five independent weeklies — *L'Expression, Le Messager, Mutations, Dikalo* and *La Plume du Jour* — were seized by police on 18 August following the publication of a conversation between economy and finance minister, Edouard Akame Mfoumou, and Ahamadou Ali, secretary general in the office of the president. The conversation touched on dissension within the government. (RSF)

Recent publication: *Ethnic Minority Rights Under Attack* (AI, July 1997, 21pp)

CHECHNYA

Vice-president Vakha Arsanov has said he will sue **Igor Malashenko**, president of Russia's independent NTV channel, over allegations on 19 August that he was the brains behind a 'highly-developed kidnapping machine' which, according to ITAR-Tass, is reponsible for some of the 1,000 hostages currently being held in the republic. The dispute followed the release on 17-18 August of two employees of the VID production company and a three-person crew from NTV, led by war correspondent **Yelena Masyuk**. Malashenko said NTV had paid over US$1 million for the lives of Masyuk, **Ilya Mordyukov** and **Dimitry Olchev**, who were seized on 10 May. Aslan Mashkadov, the Chechen leader, asserted that the journalists owed their rescue to a Chechen intervention squad, a claim derided by **Boris Berezovsky**, deputy secretary of the Security Council and an investor in *Nezavisimaya Gazeta*, the weekly *Ogonek* and ORT TV. Berezovsky said the journalists' release was due to Russia's intelligence, earning him a public rebuke from Yeltsin, due to meet Mashkadov for talks in September. (*International Herald Tribune*, RFE/RL)

CHINA

The new Hong Kong paper *Xianggang Tequ Bao* (Hong Kong Special Administrative Region Daily) was declared illegal in Guangdong Province on 5 July, on the grounds that it had failed to file a proper application with the central and local authorities. (SWB)

Over 3,000 publications have been seized so far this year in the campaign to eliminate illegal publishing and encourage publishing houses to produce books that respond more closely to the demands of the party and the Chinese people. **Yang Muzhi**, deputy director of the Press and Publications Administration, announced on 18 July that five publishing houses had been closed down, one permanently. (SWB, Xinhua news agency).

Nine Muslim separatists were executed in Xinjiang for their role in recent anti-Chinese riots which left nine dead, the local authorities announced on 28 July. A report published on 22 July by the US State Department accused China of violating the constitutional right to freedom of worship. The report was prepared at the request of the US Congress which is seeking a policy instrument to penalise religious persecution. (*Guardian, Financial Times, The Times*)

Government agencies are seeking out censorship software for use on the Internet, it was reported in early August. Technology currently in development can hold lists of thousands of blocked sites. It will allow a more flexible approach to censorship and provide privileged users with access to a broader range of information. (*South China Morning Post*)

Under new regulations issued on 20 August, foreign investment in domestic radio and television is to be banned. The ruling, which takes effect on 1 September, also covers the language and content of programmes and adver-tisements. (Reuters)

Wrath of Heaven, the book detailing in fictional form the corruption scandal in 1995 which brought down former Beijing mayor Chen Xitong and led to the suicide of his deputy Wang Baosen, was banned throughout the mainland in mid-August. Unnamed sources, cited by Reuters, gave as the reason for the ban 'the need for secrecy when public information poses a threat to the power of the Chinese collective leadership.' In May six people were arrested in connection with the publication and distribution of the novel, but author **Chen Fang**, a former magazine editor, is not expected to face prosecution. It is speculated in Hong Kong, where the book is still on sale, that he enjoys party protection. News of the ban emerged only days after the announcement that **Chen Xiaotong**, son of the disgraced mayor, had been sentenced to 12 years for his part in a US$24 million embezzlement case. (*International Herald Tribune*, Reuters, HRW/Asia)

Recent publication: *China: Death Penalty Log, Parts I-III* (AI, July 1997, 216pp)

COLOMBIA

Files and archives of the Association of Relatives of the Detained and Disappeared in Medellín were destroyed in a bomb attack on 24 June, just as key cases, in which members of the armed forces and paramilitary organisations

are implicated, reached the courts. (AI)

Public interest groups, the International Catholic Communications Organ-ization and the Social Foundation of Colombia, co-ordinated protests against a mid-July proposal by the National Commission for Television (CNTV) to regulate over 300 community television broadcasters. Under the proposals, community stations will be restricted to cable broadcasting; prevented from airing news or opinion pieces; and limited to donations and cable subscriptions for their financial backing. (AMARC)

National TV channels Cadena 1 and Cadena A face difficulties under a new law, partially enacted by the Constitutional Court on 30 July. The channels' broadcasting licences, granted in 1991, allow for a further six-year renewal period starting on 1 January 1998, but Law 335 prevents this. The court, however, refused to ratify Article 10 of the law, which would have required periodic 'evaluations' of TV news. (RSF)

Recent publication: *News of a Kidnapping* by Gabriel García Márquez (Cape, 1997)

COSTA RICA

Protests by the newspaper *La Nación* forced **Laureano Castro**, director of the Anti-Drug Intelligence Bureau, to resign on 14 June following his allegations of links between the press and drug

traffickers. (*Mesoamérica*)

CUBA

Lorenzo Paez Nunez of the Independent Press Bureau of Cuba (BPIC) was sentenced to 18 months in prison on 12 July for 'contempt and defaming the national police', following accusations that he had given reports to contacts abroad about alleged human rights violations. His one day trial was conducted without legal representation, or defence witnesses. (AI, CubaNet News)

Eighty-three detentions and arrests of members of opposition and human rights groups were made in the month of July, as Havana prepared for the World Festival of Communist Youth and the anniversary of Castro's first armed incursion against Batista. These included the detention on 16 July of four members of the Internal Dissidents'Working Group for the Analysis of the Cuban Socio-Economic Situation: **Vladimiro Roca Antunes** (*Index* 8/1992), **Marta Beatriz Roque Cabello** (*Index* 4/1995, 2/1996), **Rene Gomez Manzano** and **Felix Bonne Carcaces**. Another detained member, **Odilia Collazo Valdes**, was released on 17 July. At a press conference on 27 June, the dissidents had criticised a party discussion paper, circulating in the run-up to the Fifth Congress, and presented their own document. The four have not been formally charged, but may face 15 years' imprisonment for distributing 'enemy propaganda'. Additionally, **Cuban Orthodox Renovation Party** (PCRO) President **Diosmel Rodriguez Vega** was detained on 27 July. All are being held at the Villa Marista, the Havana State Security headquarters. The PCRO's Havana Co-ordinator, **Rafael Santiago Montes**, also detained on 27 July, was released on 12 August, having been interrogated over the bombing of two Havana hotels in early July. Other subjects of recent detentions are BPIC reporter **Luis Lopez Prendes**, CubaPress reporters **Juan Antonio Sanchez**, **Odalis Curbelo Sanchez** and **Nicolas Rosario Rosabal**, all held for between one and five days in late July and early August. CubaPress co-editor **Hector Peraza Linares** (*Index* 6/1995), and **Edel Garcia** of the Centro Norte del Pais News Agency (detained on 31 July) continue to be held. Agencia Nueva Prensa reporter **Lazaro Lazo** (*Index* 4/1995, 4/1996) and independent journalist **Olance Nogueras Rofe** (*Index* 4/1996, 6/1996) left Cuba on 28 July following two years of threats and harassment. **Lazo**'s latest detention was on 22 July. **Nogueras** reportedly said on his arrival in the US that he had been asked by Cuban security police to persuade **Raul Rivero** (*Index* 2/1996), a banned poet, journalist and founder of CubaPress, to leave the island or face lengthy imprisonment. Subject to cat-and-mouse tactics, **Rivero** was detained on 28 July, released the next day, only to be re-arrested on 12 August

for 'possession of illegal documents which constitute a criminal offence'. He was re-released on 15 August. During his detention, he was reportedly told that the authorities intend to destroy CubaPress. **William Cortes** and **Efren Martinez Purgaron**, both reporters with CubaPress, were also detained on 28 July and 13 August, respectively. (CubaNet News, AI, CPJ, PEN, RSF, *Washington Post*)

DEMOCRATIC REPUBLIC OF CONGO

Kinshasa's **Kin Malebo TV station** (TKM) is to be nationalised, following the 19 June decision by Jose Kajangua, head of state-owned Radio-Television Nationale Congolaise (RTNC). Congolese radio reported that 'by taking control of this media organisation, Mr Kajangua is conforming with the dynamics of the victorious military forces' major struggle for a new outlook.' The station was formerly owned by **Ngongo Luwowo**, who is accused of diverting equipment meant for the national television station while he was information minister. TKM denies the charge, saying it has documents to prove the equipment was acquired legally. TKM will now become the RNTC's second channel. (SWB)

EGYPT

Ibrahim Issa, editor of the independent weekly *al-Doustour*, was charged on 24

June with defamation, following a complaint by transport minister Sulaiman Metualli (*Index* 1/1997). Metualli told the prosecutor that articles in the magazine on 13 March and 23 April, dealing with the wealth of government ministers, were baseless. No date has been set for Issa's trial. (RSF)

Two editors and four journalists from the Saudi-owned, London-based newspaper *al-Sharq al-Awsat* were charged on 12 July with libelling Gamal and Ala'a Mubarak, sons of the Egyptian president. The prosecution relates to an advertisement in the newspaper on 27 May promoting an article in a sister weekly paper, *al-Jadida*. The advertisement suggested Mubarak's sons had made illegal business deals. The article, however, was never printed and the issue of *al-Sharq al-Awsat* which carried the advertisement was not sold in Egypt. The trial of the journalists, only two of whom are Egyptian, began on 20 July in Cairo. (*Middle East Times*)

Magdi Hussein, editor-in-chief of the Islamic bi-weekly *al-Sha'ab*, was sentenced on 20 July to two years' imprisonment and a US$900 fine for libelling the sons of Interior Minister Hassan al-Alfi. Hussein said he plans to appeal this latest fine. Hussein has already been fined US$1,200 in January and sentenced to a year's imprisonment for slandering the al-Alfi family (*Index* 2/1997). (*Middle East Times*)

Imprisoned novelist **Ala'a**

Hamed tried to kill himself with a razor on 3 August during an appeal court hearing to determine whether Hamed's sentence of one year in jail and a US$60 fine (*Index* 4/1997) should be suspended pending his appeal to Egypt's highest court, the Court of Cassation. Sources said Hamed hoped the judges would suspend the sentence indefinitely, but they froze it only temporarily. Hamed was released on bail pending a final ruling. In May, Hamed was convicted of producing and possessing printed materials of an indecent nature and which encourage immorality, a reference to his collection of short stories, *al-Firash* (The Bed). (PEN, A19, Reuters)

The continued detention of journalist **Hamdien Sabbahi** was condemned as a clear violation of freedom of opinion and expression at a meeting of more than 40 African and international human rights organisations in Burkina Faso on 7 August. Sabbahi and three others were detained on 17 June (*Index* 4/1997) for organising opposition to the highly controversial land law, due to be implemented in October. (Egyptian Organization for Human Rights, AI, OMCT)

Sayyed Ahmad al-Tokhi, a lawyer for the Egyptian Organization for Human Rights (EOHR), was detained on 9 August as he tried to board a flight to the United Arab Emirates. Two days later he was charged under Article 86 (bis) of the Egyptian Penal Code with crimes including 'verbally promoting ideas that contradict the fundamental principles of the ruling regime, and inciting opposition to the authorities'. He was ordered to be detained for 15 days pending inquiries. The EOHR believes al-Tokhi's detention is in connection with his attendance at a June conference discussing the new land law. (Egyptian Organization for Human Rights)

On 17 August, police confiscated copies of the book *God of this Time* by **Sayed al-Qemni** from the Madbouli al-Sagheer bookshop in northern Cairo. In a hearing the following day, prosecutors told the North Cairo Court that the book, published in September 1996, had been condemned by the Islamic Research Academy of al-Azhar as showing contempt for the Prophet Youssef and for Caliph Othman Ben Affan. Excerpts from the book have appeared in Egyptian and other Arab newspapers during the past five years. (Egyptian Organization for Human Rights)

Recent publication: *The Egyptian Predicament: Islamists, the State and Censorship* (A19, August 1997, 100pp)

ETHIOPIA

A new Amharic-language opposition radio station Radio Voice of One Free Ethiopia, began transmitting on 18 June on Wednesdays and Sundays. The station has a Washington DC mailing address but, like two other short-lived opposition stations — the Voice of Ethiopian Patriotism and Free Radio Voice of Ethiopian Unity — is apparently being beamed from one of the former Soviet republics in central Asia. (SWB)

GERMANY

On 17 August, the Federal Constitutional Court upheld a ban on a rally in Wunsiedel commemorating the tenth anniversary of the death of Hitler's deputy, Rudolf Hess. German police detained around 200 people suspected of travelling to illegal rallies in neighbouring Denmark, where more liberal freedom of speech laws allowed neo-Nazis to mark Hess's death publicly. (*Independent*, Reuters)

Recent publication: *Continuing Pattern of Police Ill-Treatment* (AI, July 1997, 43pp)

GUATEMALA

Newsreader **Norman Homero Hernandez Perez**, of Radio Campesina in Tiquisate, Escuintla, and messenger **Haroldo Escobar Noriega** were shot dead on 16 July as they left the station following completion of their early morning shifts. The motive for the attack is unknown. (CPJ, PEN)

GUINEA

Ousmane Camara, publications director of the independent magazine *l'Oeil*, and **Louis Celestin**, its editor-in-chief, were arrested on 1 August and charged with 'spreading false information' and defamation, following a complaint by minister of justice Zogbelemou Togba, who was criticised in two articles in the 25 June and 2 July editions. Despite being granted an official release on 6 August, the two remain in detention. (RSF)

HUNGARY

On 18 June, the Municipal Court in Budapest banned the publication, sale, delivery, free distribution or presentation to the public of Hitler's autobiography, *Mein Kampf,* under the provisions of the press law. Last November, the prosecutor-general's office suspended publication of the book and advised the courts to ban it. Translator **Aron Monus,** who also represents the publisher, said he will appeal. Publication of Nazi literature has been illegal in Hungary since the end of World War II. (ICFJ)

It was announced on 13 August that state security files will be opened from 1 September to researchers and Hungarian citizens who believe they were under surveillance by the state during the Communist era. It is estimated that the security services had files on 160,000 people. (RFE/RL)

INDIA

Police assaulted **Surinder Singh Oberoi,** Agence France-Presse correspondent in Kashmir, as he and 20 other journalists assembled in front of the UN office in Srinagar on 27 June to cover a demonstration by Kashmiri

separatists. Oberoi was reportedly attacked after he had asked journalist **Tauseef Mustafa** to photograph police beating two women protesters. A group of 40 journalists later protested Oberoi's beating outside the office of chief minister Farooq Abdullah. When the journalists demanded to see the chief minister, police were ordered to disperse the crowd with tear gas and batons. The minister eventually apologised for what had happened, but no officers were disciplined for the assaults. (HRW/Asia, CPJ, RSF)

On 7 July 40 men stormed into the Bangalore office of *Asian Age,* stabbed two journalists and chopped off the thumb of a guard. The mob then smashed and burned computers and office equipment. They were apparently angered by a news report about a poster in a West Bank town that depicted the prophet Mohammed as a pig. It is not clear why the mob targeted *Asian Age,* since most media in the region had reported the incident. (RSF)

Habib-ullah Naqash, photographer with *Asian Age* in Srinagar, was stopped and beaten by two policemen at a checkpoint on 27 July, while en route to cover the visit to Kashmir of Prime Minister Inder Kumar Gujral. On 8 August, **Mukhtar Ahmed,** a CNN correspondent and reporter for the Indian *Telegraph,* along with photographer **Arshad Ahmed,** were beaten by a police officer when they were stopped on their way to an

army press conference in Srinagar. Also in early August, the Indian army raided the house of **Ahmed Ali Fayaz,** bureau chief of the *Excelsior* newspaper in Budgam, 30 kilometres from Srinagar. (CPJ)

On 13 August immigration authorities refused **Martin Sugarman** permission to enter India for the purpose of reporting events in Kashmir. Sugarman, an independent photographer and film-maker, had been issued with a visa on 16 July by the Indian Consulate in San Francisco. Sugarman's passport was temporarily seized and he was questioned for several hours before being put on a plane back to London. Sugarman is the author of the book *Kashmir: Paradise Lost.* (CPJ)

On 15 August, India's Independence Day, Pamela Rook's film, *Train to Pakistan,* was denied broadcast permission by the Central Board of Film Certification (CBFC), shortly before its scheduled showing by Star TV. The story, based on a Khushwant Singh novel, concerns communal tension in a Punjabi village during India's partition. The CBFC asked the director to remove the word 'Muslim', which recurs throughout the screenplay, and all indirect references to Mahatama Gandhi. (*Indian Express*)

Recent publications: *Submission to the Human Rights Committee Concerning Implementation of Articles of the International Covenant on Civil and Political Rights* (AI, July

1997, 83pp); *The 'Enron Project' in Maharashtra: Protests Suppressed in the Name of Development* (AI, July 1997, 17pp)

IRAN

According to reports in early July, Iranian authorities have still failed to launch a thorough investigation into the death of **Ebrahim Zalzadeh** (*Index* 3/1997), former editor of the monthly literary magazine *Me'yar* (Standard) and owner of *Ebtekar* (Initiative). His family reported him missing in February and he was found one month later in a Tehran morgue. (PEN)

The Islamic Human Rights Commission announced on 15 July that **Faraj Sarkoohi** (*Index* 6/1996, 1/1997, 2/1997, 3/1997, 4/1997), imprisoned editor of *Adineh*, will finally be given an open trial and authentic legal representation. Sarkoohi had been accused of spying — a charge which carries the death penalty in Iran — but Ahmed Ebrahimi of the Iranian Pen Centre in Exile says an open trial signals the authorities' willingness to avoid the death penalty, without losing face. (*Iran News*, Iranian Pen Centre in Exile, Reuter)

The screening of four films by the Iranian director **Mohsen Makhmalbaf** at the Jerusalem Film Festival was denounced by Iran's Farabi Cinema Foundation on 16 July as 'a plot hatched by Europe and the illegal state of Israel'. The foundation, which controls much of Iran's film industry, said the showings were 'open arts banditry, and... incompatible with the most basic principles of international and cultural regulations.' It was not clear if the distributor of the films — *Gabbeh, A Moment of Innocence, Time of Love* and *Salaam Cinema* — had to obtain prior permission from Farabi for showings outside Iran. (*Middle East Times*, Reuters)

On 20 July, the official news agency IRNA reported that a Tehran court had fined the publisher of the hardline Islamic weekly *Sobh* (Morning) the equivalent of US$1,666 for 'scandalous reporting' and suspended the publication for a month. The magazine had accused minister of telecommunications Mohammed Gharazi of favouritism in delivering telephone lines, breach of budgetary guidelines, questionable practices in granting foreign contracts and wasting ministry funds on chartered air travel. A week earlier, *Sobh's* editor, **Mehdi Nassiri**, was found not guilty of libel, but guilty of insulting the minister. (Reuters)

Recent publiation: *Iran: Open Letter from Amnesty Intenational to His Excellency Hojjatoleslam val Moslemin Sayed Mohammed Khatami on the Occasion of his Inauguration as President* (AI, August 1997, 4pp)

ISRAEL

Publicity about **Mordechai Vanunu**, the nuclear technician jailed in 1986 for exposing Israel's secret atomic weapons programme, increased as the eleventh anniversary of his kidnapping by the security services approached. A partly-censored letter from Vanunu to Arab Knesset delegate, **Azmi Bishara**, was published in the daily *Yediot Aharonot* on 22 June, prompting the government to introduce legislation permitting full censorship in letters written by 'security risks' to their democratic representatives.

In mid-July, the Jerusalem Film Festival screened *I Am Your Spy*, by the Israeli director **Dani Verte**, a documentary on Vanunu. The film portrays Vanunu as a prisoner of conscience: the festival committee hesitated for weeks before agreeing to screen it. In another surprise development, Asher and Meir Vanunu met their brother face-to-face for the first time in a decade. In previous visits, warders had placed a metal screen between Vanunu and his brothers. (*Other Israel,* Israeli Council for Israeli-Palestinian Peace, *Guardian*)

Prime Minister Benyamin Netanyahu said on 7 July that he was 'deeply sorry' for the offence caused to Christians by an illustration depicting the Virgin Mary with a cow's head that appeared in the Israeli science magazine *Galileo*. The picture accompanied an article on the prospect of human cloning. (*Jerusalem Times*)

Israel began jamming broadcasts by the **Voice of Palestine** (VOP) in the West Bank and Gaza Strip on 4

August. The decision to begin the jamming, taken by the Israeli cabinet on 31 July, was initially held up due to resistance from the Israeli broadcasting authority. The cabinet said that VOP broadcasts had incited the anti-Israeli violence which culminated in 30 July's double suicide bombing in Jerusalem. (CPJ)

Recent publications: *Annual Report 1996* (Physicians for Human Rights, August 1997, 16pp); *The Quiet Deportation: Revocation of Residency of East Jerusalem Palestinians* (B'Tselem, April 1997, 38pp); *A Policy of Discrimination — Land Expropriation, Planning and Building in Jerusalem* (B'Tselem, January 1997, 126pp)

JAPAN

The education ministry came under attack in early July for its latest round of textbook censorship, part of its four-yearly policy of screening elementary, junior and high school books. Four textbooks were considered inappropriate for 'not giving enough attention to fostering good family life'. Material on the changed family structure, grandparents living separately, common law marriages and changing family member roles, was judged improper. (*Asahi Evening News*)

JORDAN

Jordan's only satirical weekly, *Abed Rabbouh*, ceased printing in late June as a result of the press law amendments introduced on 17 May (*Index*

4/1997). At least six other weeklies have been hard hit. *Al-Hayat, al-Sayyad* and *al-Bilad* have merged in order to comply with the requirement that all publications must be backed with US$420,000 in capital. *Al-Meethaq* halted publication on 9 July, but was expected to meet its financial requirements by the 15 August deadline, as was *al-Majd*. *Sawt al-Mar'a* ceased publishing for three weeks, but is reported to have found sufficient capital. *Shihan* is insulated by the wealth of the daily *al-Arab al-Youm*. The Islamist paper *al-Sabeel* is not expected to make drastic moves to comply with the law. On 8 July the Muslim Brotherhood announced that it plans to boycott the autumn general election in protest at the press law amendments. Four leftist parties joined the boycott on 20 July, and called on the six other left-wing and Arab Nationalist parties to follow suit. (RSF, Reuters, *Middle East International*)

Nazih Chawahine, a journalist on the daily *al-Arad al-Youm*, was detained by police on 24 July for having published an article on a bush fire which he titled 'The park of burned peace in Bakoura'. Bakoura was captured by Israel but returned to Jordan under the terms of the 1994 peace treaty, since when it has become known as 'the island of peace'. In March, a Jordanian soldier shot dead seven Israeli schoolgirls in the same district. (RSF)

KENYA

Jennifer Wachie, a

photographer with the *East Africa Standard*, was beaten by police on 4 July while documenting riots by students of Nairobi University against a proposed Higher Education Bill. (NDIMA)

Wafula Buke, Morris Ochieng and another man were arrested in Mombasa on 4 July for distributing leaflets that called for a strike demanding constitutional and legal reform. They have been charged with publishing false statements 'likely to cause fear and alarm to the public'. (AI)

At least nine people were killed when police and security forces broke up pro-democracy rallies in Nairobi, Kisumu, Mombasa and Nakuru on 7 July. Opposition groups had called the rallies to pressure President Daniel arap Moi to allow free access to the media, overhaul the state-appointed electoral commission and repeal colonial-era public order laws which regulate political assemblies. Journalists covering the rallies also came under attack. **Osman Njuguna**, correspondent with the All-Africa Press services, was beaten by police, as was **Peter Karuri**, a freelance photographer attached to the *Nation*. **Vitalis Musebe**, head of news at Kenya Television Network (KTN), and his deputy, **Isaiya Kabira**, were indefinitely suspended on 9 July by the KTN board as a result of their coverage. The suspensions were reduced to one month on 17 July. (Reuters, AI, NDIMA)

The National Council of

Churches of Kenya, publisher of the newspaper *Target*, is being sued by Co-operative Bank chairman Hosea Kiplagat for alleged defamation following an article linking him to a sugar import group, it was reported on 11 July. (NDIMA)

Recent publication: *Juvenile Injustice: Police Abuse and Detention of Street Children in Kenya* (HRW/Africa, June 1997, 155pp)

KYRGYZSTAN

On 5 August the Supreme Court aquitted **Zamira Sydykova** (*Index* 5/1995), chief editor of *Res Publica* weekly, of charges that she defamed Dastan Sarygulov in an article in 1993. **Aleksandr Alyantchikov**, her co-defendant, had an 18-month sentence handed down in June commuted to a suspended 12-month term. Sarygulov, manager of the state-owned gold mining company, refused to give evidence at the libel trial in 1995 when Sydykova was sentenced to 18 months. She spent two and a half months on remand. The court determined she had been guilty of libel, but dismissed the remainder of the sentence. (Bureau on Human Rights and Rule of Law)

Ramazan Ozturk, a Turkish journalist with the Istanbul-based daily *Sabah*, was prevented from entering the country upon his arrival at Bishkek airport on 9 August. Ozturk insisted on calling the Kyrgyz embassy in Turkey, but police broke his camera and

sent him back to Turkey on the plane on which he had arrived. According to police, Oztuk was barred at the insistence of Russian Federation intelligence. In February 1996 Ozturk and a colleague secretly entered Chechnya to interview the rebels, since when he has become persona non grata with the Russian authorities. (International Press Institute, RSF)

LEBANON

Lebanese journalist **Roger Nahra** was released on 6 August after a month's detention incommunicado. He was arrested by Israeli soldiers on 3 July, along with brothers Joseph and Michel and their cousin Jean, at their homes in Israeli-occupied south Lebanon. Joseph and Jean were released in mid-August but Michel, a retired policeman, still remains in detention. Since 1994 Roger Nahra has worked in south Lebanon as a reporter for Lebanese broadcasters MTV and Sawt al-Sha'ab Radio and the newspapers *al-Liwa* and Dubai's *al-Khalij*. No explanation has been given for the detention of the Nahras, but Roger said he believed it was related to his reporting. (AI, RSF)

Recent publication: *Israel's Forgotten Hostages — Lebanese Detainees in Israel and Khiam Detention Centre* (AI, July 1997, 26pp)

LESOTHO

The 15-21 July edition of *Mopheme* reports that two

journalists, *Mopheme*'s **Khutliso Sekoati** and **Christopher Shale** of *Moeletsi oa Basotho* have been targeted for assassination by state agents. *Mopheme* quotes intelligence sources as saying: 'This is in a bid to clear elements suspected to be against Prime Minister Ntsu Mokhehle and his supporters.' Lesotho police declined to comment. (MISA)

LIBYA

Recent publication: *Gross Human Rights Violations amid Secrecy and Isolation* (AI, June 1997, 36pp)

MACEDONIA

Radio Macedonia noted on 11 August that, following the collapse of the TAT pyramid investment scheme, threats to journalists and TV crews have increased to such an extent that their work is being hampered. **Nikola Talevski**, a Macedonian TV correspondent, is the most recent journalist to receive a death threat for 'biased' reporting. The Internal Macedonian Revolutionary Party-Democratic Party for Macedonian National Unity has threatened to bomb his car. (SWB)

MALAWI

The poet Jack Mapanje has called on the democratically-elected government to repeal the 1968 **Censorship Act**, the privately-owned *Nation* reported on 28 July. (MISA)

Fifteen journalists were severely beaten at police

headquarters on 11 August, following their attendance at a press conference by the opposition Movement for Independence, Rebirth and African Integration (MIRIA) in Bamako. **Yero Diallo**, director of the magazine *Le Tambour*, was hospitalised, with severe injuries to the head and spine. **Basse Diarra** of the government-controlled *L'Essor* sustained knee injuries, while BBC correspondent, **Said Penda**, was assaulted and had equipment damaged. The journalists were released after two hours. (Reuters, SWB)

Recent publication: *Broadcasting Law in Malawi* (Civil Liberties Committee/A19, Febuary 1997, 15pp)

MAURITANIA

The interior ministry banned the newspapers *al Bouchra* and *La Vérité* in late June. The ban followed a police raid on the newspapers' offices on 23 June, in which personal property and documentation were confiscated. The raids are the first time the police have seized property from Mauritanian newspapers. Paradoxically, both newspapers, which belong to the same publishing group, are noted supporters of the government. (RSF, SWB)

MEXICO

On 3 June **Gerardo Gonzalez Figueroa**, chair of the coalition Co-ordination of Non-Governmental Organisations for Peace, received the latest in a series of death threats against his children.

Similar threats were made in November 1996 and May 1997 (*Index* 4/1997). (AAASHRAN)

On 15 July **Benjamín Flores González**, editor and owner of *La Prensa* newspaper in San Luis Rio Colorado, Sonora State, became the twenty-third journalist to be murdered in Mexico since 1984. He was ambushed outside his office by four men in a car, then shot 17 times with an AK-47 assault rifle before receiving three shots to the head from a .22 calibre pistol. Recipient of several death threats prior to his murder, González continued to publish articles on the alleged involvement of local government officers and police with drug traffickers, including the Sinaloa cartel. (AI, CPJ)

MOLDOVA

Adrian Usatai, head of state radio and **Dumitru Turcanu**, director of national television, were dismissed by parliament on 24 July, accused of violating constitutional provisions on political pluralism and providing inaccurate information. But another factor in Usatai's dismissal was the broadcast last November of a secretly-recorded telephone conversation between deputy **Nicolae Andronic** and Moldova's former ambassador to Germany, **Alexandru Buruiana**. (RFE/RL)

NAMIBIA

The media was barred by the ruling South West Africa

People's Organisation (SWAPO) from covering the party's second congress at the end of June. (*Southern African Report*)

President Sam Nujoma banned the holding of all public demonstrations without police permission, after former fighters against apartheid rule took some government officials hostage on 8 July. The ban was denounced as 'illegal' and 'unconstitutional' by legal commentators. (MISA)

NEPAL

On 31 July **Om Sharma**, correspondent for the newspapers *Maya Morcha* and *Rabibar Weekly*, was arrested during a police raid on his home in Kathmandu. The police confiscated personal documents, and later searched the offices of *Maya Marcha*. Sharma was last reported in custody at Hanuman Dhoka police station. No reason has been given for his arrest. (RSF)

NICARAGUA

Daniel Ortega, secretary general of the Sandinista National Liberation Front (FSLN), may be charged with sedition following remarks made in a television interview on 20 June when he suggested the FSLN might overthrow President Arnoldo Alemán. Ortega's remarks were inspired by the National Assembly's consideration of an anti-protest bill introduced by the governing Liberal Alliance party on 4 June. The bill proposes criminal penalties for participation in public demonstrations and protests, with mandatory jail sentences of six months. (*Mesoamérica*)

The government has indefinitely suspended the granting of frequencies and operating licences for radio broadcasters, and is accused of jamming independent radio transmissions in Managua, via the state telecommunications company, TELCOR. Disrupted transmissions include the live broadcast of a student protest on 26 June, calling for the government to transfer the constitutionally-enshrined 6 per cent (US$36 million) of the national budget to higher education. (AMARC)

NIGER

A new press law was passed in late June to license journalists and criminalise the offences of defamation and insulting the president. It provides for sentences of two to five years' imprisonment. Only journalists who have graduated from journalism school or been in the profession for five years will be entitled to the new 'press card'. (RSF)

NIGERIA

Bayo Awogbemi, assistant editor of *Nigerian Tribune*, and **Abiodun Mudashiru**, a reporter with Independent Television (ITV), were arrested on 30 June for writing articles about a clash between religious cults at the University of Benin. Awogbemi was charged in court on 11 July, but Mudashiru was released on 2 July after ITV broadcast a

retraction. Awogbemi had been previously arrested in March, as had **Emman Amaize**, correspondent for the *Vanguard,* over a story headlined: 'Fresh human skull found in a school'. (*Media Monitor*)

Chief Oni Egbunine, publisher of Owerri-based *Horn Newspapers*, was beaten into a coma on 1 July by soldiers at the Imo State Government House. The military authorities are said to have been irritated by the publication of a story titled 'Imo Estacode Fraud' in the 26 June edition of the *Horn*. The article alleged corruption by officials in the state government. (*Media Monitor*)

The draft constitution, upon which next year's proposed transition to civil rule is to be based, establishes a National Mass Media Commission, whose functions are set out in section 46 of part one of the third schedule of the constitution. Section 46(3) prohibits the circulation of private media companies beyond the state in which they are based. The commission says that it intends to protect individuals from media intimidation and prevent unwarranted enquiries into a person's private life without their express consent. (*Media Monitor*)

Ben-Charles Obi, the former *Classique* editor currently serving a 15-year sentence at Agodi prison in Ibadan, is suffering from an ailment suspected to be a disease of the nervous system. **George

Mbah**, former assistant editor of *Tell*, is also sick. (*Media Monitor*)

Mohammed Adamu, the Abuja correspondent of *African Concord* magazine, was arrested on 27 July. No reason was given for the arrest. It is speculated that it is connected with the 14 July cover story: 'Mustapha — ruthless man behind Abacha'. Hamza Mustapha is General Sani Abacha's security chief. (Reuters, RSF, *Media Monitor*)

Sunday Olaniran, a journalist with the *Daily Sketch* was reported missing on 1 August. (*Media Monitor*)

The publisher of the *Oriwu Sun*, **Monsur Olowosago**, was attacked by unknown persons at a ceremony at Ijehu-Ode, Ogun State on 7 August. They reportedly told him that a past chairman of Ikorodu local government was unhappy with a story published about corruption. 'We will teach you,' the attackers reportedly said, 'that it is not every thing that the eyes see, that the mouth talks about.' (*Media Monitor*)

Recent publications: *Unshackling the Nigerian Media: An Agenda for Reform* (A19/Media Rights Agenda); *Special and Military Tribunals and the Administration of Justice in Nigeria* edited by Festus Okoye (Human Rights Monitor, 1997, 297pp)

PAKISTAN

Khaliq Kiani, correspondent for *Business Recorder* in Karachi, was assaulted on 11

July by two unidentified motorcyclists near Melody Market, while walking toward Aabpara. Kiani had been filing investigative stories about bureaucrats who were recently suspended by the government. (CPJ, Ansar Burney Welfare Trust)

On 16 July the Federal Investigative Agency (FIA) raided the offices of private radio station FM-100 in Islamabad and Shaheen Pay TV (SPTV) Karachi, arresting five executives at the two outlets, including directors, **Mohammed Ali Pasha** and **Abbas Rizvi**. Pasha and Rizvi were taken to Islamabad for interrogation by the Special Investigative Unit, reportedly on orders from the *Ehtesab* (Accountability) Cell, based at the prime minister's secretariat in Islamabad. Both companies have been charged with violating clauses of the private channel agreement. But the FIA has also sealed the records which would, allegedly, incriminate **Javed Pasha**, chairman of both FM-100 and SPTV, in the illegal acquisition of licences in 1995. Now living in the UK, Javed Pasha reportedly obtained his permits after Asif Ali Zardari, husband of former Prime Minister Benazir Bhutto, had applied personal pressure. SPTV and FM-100 are allowed to air programmes until a decision is taken by higher authorities. (RSF, Ansar Burney Welfare Trust)

The Karachi offices of the daily *Ummat* and weekly *Takbeer* newspapers were raided by police from Al-Fatah police station on 16

July. Police sources said that the raid was an unsuccessful bid to arrest *Takbeer*'s editor **Sarwat Jamal Asmi**, reporter **Shah Rukh Hasan** and the editor of *Ummat*, **Rafiq Afghan**, who had allegedly published an article which provoked the killing of the two sons, guard and driver of deputy superintendant of police Aziz-ur-Rehman. (Ansar Burney Welfare Trust)

Shakeel Naich, reporter for the Sindhi-language daily *Awami Awaz*, suffered serious head injuries in an attack by members of the Sindh National Front (SNF) on 3 August. Naich had written an article critical of the former caretaker chief minister of Sindh, Mumtaz Bhutto, who is also the chief of the SNF and uncle of former Prime Minister Benazir Bhutto. (Pakistan Press Foundation, CPJ)

PALESTINE (AUTONOMOUS AREAS)

Fathi Ahmed Subuh, an education professor at Gaza's al-Azhar university, was detained on 2 July by officers of the Palestinian Preventive Security Service (PSS). Subuh had given an exam to students on 21 June asking them to analyse administrative corruption at the university and within the Palestinian Authority. Subuh's detention belongs to an apparent pattern of intimidating Palestinian intellectuals. **Imad Faisal Sabi**, an economist, has been detained since 12 December 1995 for his public opposition to the Oslo peace accords. In late May, Palestinian-

American journalist **Daoud Kuttab** and al-Azhar lecturer **Ayyub Uthman** were each detained for about a week (*Index* 4/1997). (Palestinian Human Rights Monitoring Group)

Jewish settler **Tatiana Susskind** was brought before an east Jerusalem court on 19 July for pasting posters depicting the prophet Mohammed as a pig on to 20 Palestinian stores in Hebron on 27 June. The posters drew violent protests in which around 100 Palestinians were injured. Israeli soldiers wounded six journalists covering the affrays: Reuters cameraman **Mazen Dana**, Reuters photographer **Rula Halawani**, an Associated Press photographer and cameramen for AP, Abu Dhabi Television and the US network ABC. (Reuters, *Middle East International, Jerusalem Times*)

Recent publications: *Joint Report on the 1996 Palestinian Elections* (al-Haq/A19/ICJ, May 1997, 131pp); *Plunder, Destruction and Despoilation: An Analysis of Israel's Violations of the International Law of Cultural Property in the Occupied West Bank and Gaza Strip* (al-Haq, May 1997, 97pp); *The Right to Freedom of Assembly: An Analysis of the Position of the Palestinian National Authority* (al-Haq, March 1997, 63pp); *Reconstruction of the Events of Late September 1996 in the West Bank and the Gaza Strip* (al-Haq, 1997, 18pp); *Lethal Training: The Killing of Muhammad al-Hilu by Undercover Soldiers in Hizmeh Village* (B'Tselem, March 1997, 12pp)

PANAMA

The National University has instituted disciplinary proceedings against two professors under its newly enacted ethics code. **Miguel Antonio Bernal** and **Federico Ardila** face expulsion from their posts for publicly requesting an audit of the university's administrative affairs by Panama's comptroller in January. Also a radio show host, Bernal had broadcast comments on the government's alleged attempts to stifle discussion within the university on the future of US bases in Panama. (HRW/ Americas)

Gustavo Gorriti, the Peruvian-born associate editor of opposition newspaper *La Prensa,* was refused a renewal of his work permit on 4 August by Labour Minister Mitchell Doens, who was named in one of Gorriti's stories. Gorriti, who was forced to leave Peru under pressure from the Fujimori administration in 1992, heads *La Prensa*'s investigative unit and has pursued stories relating to President Perez Balladares' receipt of campaign donations from Colombian drug trafficker, José Castrillon Henao. (CPJ, RSF)

PERU

According to the Office of Human Rights of Journalists (OFIP) in Lima, 56 attacks on journalists and media outlets had been recorded in Peru by the end of June 1997. On 8 July, Congress president Victor Joy Way said greater protection for journalists, particularly those who cover politics, would be forthcoming from the ministry of the interior. Pointing out the contradiction in this position, the Institute for Press and Society noted that it is the interior minister, General Cesar Saucedo, who has recently gone on the offensive against **Baruch Ivcher** (*Index* 3/1997, 4/1997).

The Ivcher case is fast turning into a constitutional crisis. On 14 July the state-sponsored *El Peruano* announced that Ivcher, who owns Frecuencia Latina/ Channel 2 television station and is currently taking refuge in Miami, was to be stripped of his citizenship. This effectively prevents him from owning a stake in his own stations. Earlier this year, Channel 2 aired programmes critical of the security forces' human rights abuses, as well as an exposé of phone-tapping of journalists and public figures by the National Intelligence Service (SIN).

On 15 July, four Congress members lodged constitution-based accusations against the interior minister and defence minister General Tomas Castillo Meza. Journalists such as **Gustavo Mohme** of the opposition daily *La Republica* and correspondents of the tabloid *Ojo* have expressed solidarity with Ivcher despite physical threats, such as the attempted kidnapping of **Luis Angeles Laynes**, *Ojo's* political editor on 1 July.

By 17 July three government ministers had resigned in protest: foreign minister Francisco Tudela; defence minister General Tomas Castillo Meza; and justice minister Carlos Hermoza. Two others have since followed. On 1 August Ivcher's shares in Channel 2 were 'suspended' by the state on the grounds that he is no longer a Peruvian national. On 3 August, Channel 2 broadcast conversations of former UN secretary general, Javier Perez de Cuellar, who leads opposition coalition, and his supporters and family, which were made by SIN phone-tappers before and after the April 1995 election campaign. De Cuellar has condemned the government's continuing harassment of Ivcher, and said that Peru is 'living in a permanent coup d'etat'. Meanwhile, thousands of supporters surrounded the Channel 2 building and journalists are sleeping at the station. (AI, IFJ/FIP, *Guardian, International Herald Tribune*, Institute for Press and Society, *Peru Update*)

POLAND

TV producer **Lech Dymarski** was suspended on 23 July for breaking the guidelines for the Pope's visit in June. According to Ryszard Miazek, chairman of Polish TV, Dymarski had screened a programme on the dispute between Rome and Warsaw over the ratification of Poland's Concordat with the Vatican. Instructions had been given that there should be no programmes on sensitive, church-related issues during the visit. Dymarski's programme provoked considerable controversy in Poland, and an official note of criticism from the Vatican. (SWB)

ROMANIA

On 9 July the government approved an 'urgent ordinance' to abolish provisions in the education law which stipulate that high school final exams and university entrance tests must be in the Romanian language. The amendment ensures education in the mother tongue at all levels (*Index* 4/1997). The Hungarian Federation of Romania had threatened to withdraw from the government coalition if the amendment were not implemented in time for the next school year. The Party of Romanian National Unity urged that a special parliamentary session be held to debate the ordinance, a move which was backed on 12 August by the Social Democrats. (RFE/RL)

RUSSIA

Larisa Kislinskaya, of the newspaper *Sovershenno Sekretno,* was stripped of her accreditation on 20 June for 'conduct discrediting the journalistic profession'. Her articles concerning a video, which allegedly showed justice minister Valentin Kovalyov cavorting in a sauna with scantily-clad women, forced him to return abruptly from a foreign trip. The ministry of justice claimed Kislinskaya had obtained the video from the Russian underworld, while a lawyer for Kovalyov said it was a video-montage. (SWB)

The Council on Foreign and Defence Policies, a semi-official body which includes some of President Boris Yeltsin's closest advisers, announced on 3 July the formation of a blacklist of western publications guilty of printing negative articles about Russia's economy and society. First to appear on the list were the *Washington Post, Forbes* and *La Republica* (Italy). Others under threat, according to the newspaper *Segodnya,* include *Le Monde* and the *Guardian.* Publications on the list will be denied any assistance in contacting or interviewing Russian businessmen and politicians. (SWB, *Financial Times)*

On 7 July the state-run television network RTR decided not to broadcast a series on journalism called *Chetvertaya vlast* (The Fourth Estate). The first programme, which included sections on how the Chechen rebels 'won the information war' and whether journalism is the equivalent of espionage, was scheduled for 29 June. Despite the removal of the Chechnya section, it again failed to be aired on 6 July. RTR's deputy chairman Mikhail Lesin, founder of the Video-International advertising firm, made the final decision to cancel the series. (RFE/RL)

On 22 July President Boris Yeltsin vetoed a bill from the Duma which would have severely restricted the civil rights of 'non-traditional' religious groups. The draft law was an attempt to curb the right 'to spread a belief' of groups less than 15 years old

(*Index* 4/1997). Duma speaker Gennadii Seleznev, however, predicted on 23 July that parliament would override the veto. Yeltsin warned that if this occurs, he will sign the law but publish it alongside a description of the inherent violations it entails of the international and constitutional agreements ratified by Russia. (*Guardian, Obshchaya Gazeta,* RFE/RL)

Former junior diplomat, **Platon Obukhov**, went on trial for treason on 28 July accused of giving secrets to British diplomats who were expelled from Russia last year. Obukhov, who writes best-selling spy novels, claims that he met the diplomats merely to obtain new material for his latest book. (*Independent,* Interfax)

Deputy Prime Minister Boris Nemtsov said in an interview with RFE/RL on 14 August that the state should take control of the 'ideological foundations' and finances of the Russian public television station, ORT. At present, the state has a 51 per cent stake, but security council deputy secretary **Boris Berezovski** has been the most influential figure at ORT since it began broadcasting in April 1995. (RFE/RL)

RWANDA

Georges Ruggiu, a far-right Belgian journalist, was arrested in late August by the United Nations Rwanda genocide tribunal. Ruggiu worked for Radio Milles Collines in Kigali in 1994 and is accused of making broadcasts which incited violence against ethnic Tutsis and moderate Hutus. He is the first non-Rwandan to be arrested by the tribunal. (Reuters)

SAUDI ARABIA

On 19 July the Arab telecommunications organisation, Arabsat, pulled the plug on programmes from **Canal France International** (CFI) for transmitting an 'immoral' show in Arab countries. The clampdown was prompted by the broadcast of a pornographic film. An official said that CFI had been warned before that some of its programming offended Islamic sensibilities and warned that Arabsat would now review its contract with CFI. (Reuters, *Middle East Times*)

SENEGAL

On 8 August the government suspended the private radio stations **Sud FM**, **Nostalgie** and **Dunya** for three months for non-payment of their broadcasting fees. Sud FM resumed broadcasting on 15 August. (SWB)

SERBIA-MONTENEGRO

On 26 July communications minister Dojcilo Radojevic suspended his order to shut down 76 independent radio and television stations until after Serbia's presidential and legislative elections on 21 September. The stations had been threatened with closure for failing to meet a 30 June deadline to submit the documentation necessary to secure their licences. The ministry claimed that the stations were 'a threat to public welfare' and had began to confiscate their equipment and threaten staff with criminal proceedings. On 26 July Yugoslav information minister Goran Matic conceded that the closures 'could be interpreted as an obstacle to preparations for free and fair elections'. Five banned radio and television stations resumed service on 30 June. (RFE/RL, Reuters)

The bank account of **Fininvest**, which publishes the independent daily *Nasa Borba*, was frozen by the Income Management Bureau on 29 July in a dispute over an unpaid tax fine (*Index* 4/1997). In a letter to Prime Minister Mirko Marjanovic, company chairman Dusan Malesevic said the decision had compromised the paper's ability to publish. The management had lodged a complaint over the fine, which was imposed even though a February tax inspection revealed nothing untoward. (RSF)

Srpska Rec, the newspaper of the Serbian Renewal Movement, was ordered to pay a fine of US$24,000 in early August, after losing a defamation case brought by **Marko Milosevic**, son of Yugoslav President Slobodan Milosevic. The paper was alleged to have published two articles depicting Marko Milosevic as an 'amoral, anti-social and decadent person'. (RSF)

Radio Boom 93 returned to the air on 3 August, after an eight-month hiatus following the annulment of local elections in November 1996. The station has not secured permission to operate, however. Milorad Tadici, director and chief editor, said that since all other banned radio stations had been permitted to broadcast since 26 July, Boom 93 has decided to resume operations. (SWB)

SIERRA LEONE

Shortly after the 8 July issue of the *Democrat* went on sale, soldiers from the Armed Forces Revolutionary Council (AFRC) arrived at the editorial offices and arrested seven individuals, whom they released on 19 July. *Democrat* reporter **Saloman Conteh**, freelance correspondent **Jeff Bowlay Williams** and **Fatama Kamara**, a visitor to the offices, were among those detained. (RSF, CPJ)

On 16 July the *Standard Times* announced its suspension following numerous threats from AFRC soldiers. Three weeks earlier, *For Di People* suspended publication for the same reason. On 30 July some 1,500 copies of *Standard Times* were confiscated during a raid on the editorial offices. AFRC soldiers were looking for managing editor **Philip Neville**, who went into hiding. (RSF, CPJ)

On 18 July **Martin Martins**, editor of *Business News*, was detained overnight for allegedly sending reports to ousted President Tejan

Kabbah via fax. (RSF)

Dominic Lamine, deputy editor of the private *Unity Now*, and **Sahr Mbayo**, news editor, were arrested along with two secretaries on 26 July. Editor **Frank Kposow** went into hiding. Soldiers confiscated the computer system and later claimed to have found subversive notes and documents. On 25 July *Unity Now* had published an article calling for the AFRC's immediate withdrawal. Sahr Mbayo and the two secretaries were released on 30 July, Dominic Lamine on 2 August. The wanted notice on Frank Kposowa was lifted in early August. (CPJ)

Suliman Momodu, correspondent for *Concord Times* and BBC stringer, went into hiding in late July as he was being sought by Revolutionary United Front soldiers. (CPJ)

Gibril Foday Musa, managing editor of the *New Tablet* and **Emmanuel Senessie**, one of its journalists, went into hiding from late July until the beginning of August following the burning of copies of the latest issue and the arrest of three newspaper sellers and **Suliman Janger**, the production manager. (RSF)

On 18 August, **Kelvin Lewis**, Freetown-based stringer for the Voice of America, **Ojukutu Macaulay**, editor of *Quill* and an unnamed driver were detained until 19 August. They were arrested on their way to cover a student demonstration in Freetown

and incarcerated in a shipping container at Cockrill Military Headquarters, where they were repeatedly assaulted with the blunt ends of machetes. One student was killed and 35 arrested in the demonstration. (CPJ, Reuters)

SLOVAKIA

The government announced on 2 July that it will withdraw a controversial textbook from schools, following an outcry that it denies the persecution of Slovak Jews during World War II. *The History of Slovakia and the Slovaks*, by **Milan Durica**, was written and published with funding from the European Union but its treatment of the fascist Slovak state, a puppet regime of Nazi Germany, persuaded EU external relations commissioner, Hans van den Broek, to press the government to ban it. Prime Minister Vladimir Meciar conceded that parts of the book were historically inaccurate, but he refused to ban it from bookstores. Deputies from the ultra-right Slovak National Party, a partner in the governing coalition, condemned the EU's 'censorship order', praising the book as a 'precious and objective summary of the history of Slovakia'. Of a prewar population of 70,000 Jews, less than 10,000 survived the wartime Slovak state. (Reuters)

SOLOMON ISLANDS

On 16 August Prime Minister Solomon Mamaloni halted a public discussion programme

on SIBC radio, the only source of information for the rural areas. The show featured a discussion between **Afu Billy** and **John Roughan**, both leading figures in local NGOs. Phone-in callers discussed the need to take a closer look at election candidates' records and criticised the calibre of political leadership and the islands' flagging economy. Using his powers as broadcasting minister, Mamaloni telephoned SIBC and ordered the show off the air, threatening to have those responsible arrested and to 'wreck the place up', if it were not. (Pacific Islands News Association)

SOUTH AFRICA

The South Afrian Human Rights Commission has upheld a complaint by a gay and lesbian organisation that a municipal ban on an advert which promotes their counselling and information services had violated their right to freedom of expression. The poster would have emblazoned Pretoria buses with the words 'Gay is OK... but call us anyway.' After an internal review, Pretoria City Council upheld its own ban on 2 July, arguing that the advert conflicted with 'certain religious principles'. (Freedom of Expression Institute)

On 2 July police raided the home of freelancer **Derek Fleming**, confiscating his documents and hard disk and detaining him for six days. Fleming said the action stemmed from his investigations into the

● ●

OBLATES OF SRI LANKA

On the excommunication of Fr Tissa Balasuriya OMI

The Provincial Superior of the Oblates of Sri Lanka, together with his Council and the Oblate Theology Circle, met on Thursday 16 January 1997 to assess the sad situation that has arisen by the excommunication inflicted on our brother Oblate Fr Tissa Balasuriya OMI.

Fr Tissa is a distinguished member of our Province. He worked as Rector of Aquinas College and he is the Founder-Director of the Centre for Society and Religion which has done so much for national development, inter-religious dialogue, ecumenism and justice and peace in our country. His ministry has been in line with the vision of Vatican Council II and the missionary priorities of the Oblate Congregation worldwide. His ministry has been approved and supported by his Oblate Superiors.

The initial cause of his condemnation was the so-called theological errors of his book, *Mary and Human Liberation*. It is important to note that Fr Balasuriya's intention in writing this book was 'not to dilute Marian devotion, but to make it more meaningful and truly fulfilling for all.' The process to evaluate these so-called errors began in December 1992 with the Bishops' Conference and has gone on since then through various steps.

A public statement listing these alleged errors was published in the *Catholic Messenger* and *Gnanartha Pradeepa* on 5 June 1994. Unfortunately, Fr Balasuriya's reply did not find a place in the same media. The matter was then referred to the Congregation for the Doctrine of the Faith (CDF) Rome, which sent him observations concerning these alleged errors in July 1994. His detailed response to these observations was dismissed by the CDF with a curt phrase, 'unsatisfactory'.

The CDF wished him to sign a Profession of Faith which touched many of the themes outlined in his book to assure them of his orthodoxy. Fr Balasuriya did not sign this Profession of Faith since it contained certain ambiguities, especially with regard to the people of other religions and the ordination of women to the priestly ministry.

In place of this Profession of Faith, Fr Balasuriya signed the much richer Profession of Faith of Pope Paul VI, Credo of the People of God, written after Vatican II, with the addition of the following note: 'I, Fr Tissa Balasuriya OMI make and sign this Profession of Faith of Pope Paul VI in the context of theological development and Church practice since Vatican II and the freedom and responsibility of Christians and theological searchers under Canon law.' In the Notification of Fr Balasuriya's excommunication, the CDF held that this addition rendered the Profession of Faith of Pope Paul VI defective. We feel that this note does not touch the substantial value of the Profession of Faith and expresses common methodological presuppositions of modern theologians.

● ●

• •

The CDF insisted that Fr Balasuriya should sign their version of the Profession of Faith formulated especially for him with no conditions or qualifications. He refused to do so because it would do violence to his conscience. To cut a long story short, this led to his final excommunication.

There has been some misunderstanding in this country as to the meaning of excommunication. It is a rare sanction and, in terms of the Canon Law, means only the following.

An excommunicated person is forbidden:

1. to have any ministerial part in the celebration of the Sacrifice of the Eucharist, or in other ceremonies of public worship;

2. to celebrate the sacraments or sacramentals and to receive the sacraments;

3. to exercise any ecclesiastical offices, ministries, functions or act of governance.

Nothing more is to be arbitrarily added to these.

The inflicted excommunication does not mean that Fr Balasuriya is derobed or defrocked. He continues to be an Oblate of Mary Immaculate, priest and religious and a Catholic Christian.

It is a matter of a deep sadness to note that the whole process against Fr Balasuriya has been heavily flawed from the beginning by the failure to dialogue with him. At no stage, (either in Sri Lanka or in Rome) was he given an opportunity to dialogue about his book or his alleged errors. Nor was there any inquiry at which he could answer the accusations against him. Whatever took place was by correspondence. Nor was there any dialogue between Fr Balasuriya and a Board of competent theologians. All attempts to establish a Conciliation Board in Sri Lanka to solve the question were fruitless...

In any case, the excommunication seems to us a penalty out of tune with the spirit of the Gospel which should animate us in this day and age after Vatican II. It acquires added incongruity when applied to a senior priest and religious who has contributed so much to Church and Society for the past 51 years and who passionately desires to remain within the Church.

We, therefore, insistently urge that the CDF should repeal the penalty of excommunication. Other means should be devised to deal with the alleged theological errors of this book and to place them before the international theological community and the Church.

John Camillus Fernando OMI, *Provincial Superior, Sri Lanka*
Anselm Silva OMI, *President, Oblate Theology Circle*

21 January 1997

Mary and Human Liberation, by Fr Tissa Balasuriya and with an introduction by Edmund Hill OP, is published by Mowbray, an imprint of Cassell, in October

• •

activities of Craig Kotze, communications advisor to police commissioner George Fivaz. (Freedom of Expression Institute)

Denel, the export arm of the state-controlled arms manufacturer Armscor, obtained an interim injunction from the High Court on 20 July to prevent the *Sunday Independent, Sunday Tribune* and *Sunday Argus* from publishing the name of the country involved in the biggest defence contract in South African history. Denel also laid criminal charges against the three papers, their editors and journalist **Newton Kanhema**, citing the 1968 Armaments and Production Act. On 3 August the *Sunday Independent* defied the interdict and named Saudi Arabia as the country involved. The temporary interdict and criminal charges were then individually withdrawn by the High Court at the request of Denel. (Inter Press Service, Reuters, Freedom of Expression Institute)

Business Day and the *Sunday Times* are involved in a high court application to secure the release of the full transcript of the bail hearing of **Wouter Basson**, former head of South Africa's Chemical and Biological Warfare programme. Documents confiscated at Basson's house, when he was arrested on a drugs charge, allegedly contained details of South Africa's chemical and biological warfare programme during the 1980s. (Freedom of Expression Institute)

SOUTH KOREA

Three writers of a newsletter accused of 'encouraging, praising and benefiting' North Korea — an offence which can carry a seven-year sentence under the National Security Law — have been released on bail pending their trial in March 1998. **Soh Hyoung-joon, Soh Mi-on** and **Hwang Yun-mi** are charged with publishing and distributing the weekly, which has been published since 1988 and reports on the youth organisation Nasachong, cultural events, rallies and family activities. The charges were brought in connection with three articles; one on the reunification of the two Koreas, another calling for the abolition of the National Security Law and a third on the annual 'pan-national rally'. (PEN)

SRI LANKA

On 1 July **Sinha Ranatunga**, editor of Colombo's *Sunday Times* (*Index* 2/1995, 3/1995), was found guilty on two charges of criminally defaming President Chandrika Kumaratunga. He was sentenced to 18 months in prison, plus a suspended sentence of seven years. The case was sparked by a gossip column published in February 1995. (*Daily News, The Island*)

Posts and telecommunications minister Mangala Samaraweera announced on 4 July plans to establish a media council and a new broadcasting bill. He said that the state-owned media suffered from serious credibility problems and proposed a new code of conduct for government radio and TV. The official news agency Lankapuvath would be wound up within two weeks, he said, and the electronic media revamped so as to provide fairer coverage to the opposition. The controversial Broadcasting Bill, overturned by the Supreme Court in May (*Index* 4/1997), will be redrafted by a parliamentary select committee which is to include members of the opposition. (SWB)

Iqbal Attas (*Index* 10/1993), one of Sri Lanka's leading military reporters and the 1994 winner of the CPJ's International Press Freedom Award, came under surveillance by a group of unidentified men in early July following his recent reports in Colombo's *Sunday Times* on financial irregularities in defence operations. Minister of posts, telecommunications and media, Mangala Samaraweera, told Attas that the surveillance had not been authorised by government security agencies. (CPJ)

A peaceful student demonstration in Colombo on 31 July led by the Inter-University Student Federation, was broken up by police using tear gas and water cannons. The students were protesting at proposed educational reforms which will reduce the number of subjects offered for the GCE (Advanced Level) to three, and the introduction of an 'aptitude' test for university entrance. The demonstrators claim the latter proposal is an attempt to exclude from higher education students from poor urban or rural backgrounds. (*Inform*, Free Media Movement)

SUDAN

Kamel Hassan Bakhit, editor-in-chief of *Al-Majallis*, and **Abdel Majuid Mansour**, the chairman of the board of the daily's proprietors, the Public Printing and Publications Company, were detained on 9 August by the authorities and released two days later, apparently without charge. Their detention appeared to have been triggered by an *Al-Majallis* article concerning the theft of the portable telephone owned by Brigadier Bakri Hassan Salih, Sudan's interior minister. (CPJ)

Recent publication: *A Desolate 'Peace': Human Rights in the Nuba Mountains* (African Rights, August 1997, 27pp)

SWITZERLAND

On 23 July the Swiss Bankers Association released the list of dormant bank accounts, dating back to World War II in an attempt to trace the survivors of the Holocaust or their families. Investigators have turned up more than twice as many accounts as they thought existed a year ago. The release of the names represents a radical departure for the Swiss government which has lifted secrecy laws, forcing the banks to allow their files to be searched. The move was made in response to the international outcry over claims that banks had been

blocking claims on these accounts. (*Financial Times, Independent*)

SYRIA

On 7 July **Zubayda Muqabel**, a press officer working for Syrian Vice-President Rif'at al-Assad, was detained in Damascus by members of the special security force, al-Amn al-Khass. Muqabel was reportedly taken from her car near her office. No charges have been brought against her, but she has not been permitted access to her family or a lawyer. It is not known where she is being detained. (AI)

As Syria's rapprochement with Iraq gathers pace, the government has shut down Damascus' **Voice of Free Iraq** radio station, run by Iraqi dissidents. Voice of Free Iraq had already reduced its broadcasts mainly to music and discussion programmes. The action followed the Iraqi government's closure of Amin Hafez's Voice of Arab Syria radio station, which broadcast anti-Assad programming from Baghdad. (*Independent*)

TAIWAN

Taiwan's top intelligence agency is accused of stifling the freedom of the press by bringing a criminal libel case against the daily *Independence Morning Post* for its story, published 22 July, about phone-tapping. Intelligence director, Yin Tsung-wen, ordered the bugging of phones belonging to National Assembly deputies who had opposed constitutional

amendments to reduce the power of the provincial government. Yin demanded a retraction, which the newspaper refused to provide. Editor-in-chief, Chow Mei-li claimed: 'We have the hard proof.' The editor and publisher could face jail. The preliminary hearing was on 15 August. (CPJ)

THAILAND

Bohkin Polakula, chief of the prime minister's office, told directors of the five government television channels on 7 August that they should avoid alarming the public with reports on the country's economic downturn. It is unclear whether the government intends to discourage negative financial reporting. Independent television and the newspapers have not yet been similarly approached. (*South China Morning Post*)

TIBET

A play and a guide-book on seventeenth-century Tibetan history were officially banned at the start of a new literature campaign on 11 July. The play, *Secrets of the Potala*, was produced by the Lhasa Theatre Troupe and had toured China in 1996 until its closure for 'political reasons'. (Tibet Information Network)

The use of religion in teaching materials was condemned by Chen Kuiyuan, secretary of Tibet's Communist Party, in a newspaper article on 11 July. Religion continues to be the target of China's continuing anti-separatist campaign. Political re-education teams, some of them armed, are reportedly forcing monks to provide 'correct' answers to questions set by the Supreme Politburo Standing Committee. Favoured replies include: 'The Dalai Lama is the head of the serpent' and 'the biggest obstacle to the establishment of normal order is Tibetan Buddhism'. This year, over 300 nuns and monks are reported to have sought asylum in India and Nepal. (Tibet Information Network, *The Times*)

TUNISIA

Mahmoud Boumedjeria, managing editor of the Algerian weekly *el-Kilaa*, is reported to have been tortured in late July during interrogation at the transit centre of Tunisia's el-Ouardia revolutionary guard. Boumedjeria remains in detention despite his acquittal on 15 July on charges of forging Tunisian entry and exit stamps. He was initially detained on 28 March, having fled from the violence in Algeria. Publication of *el-Kilaa* was suspended in May 1996. (RSF)

TURKEY

On 21 June a bomb exploded at the Ankara office of the left-wing daily *Halk Icin Kurtulus*. There was some damage to the building, but no-one was hurt. On 22 June a second bomb exploded at the Istanbul office of the daily *Hurriyet*. Again, there were no casualties. On 25 June unknown assailants fired shots

at the building housing the offices of the Turkish television network **Interstar**. (RSF)

MED-TV, the world's only Kurdish-language satellite TV, suffered deliberate technical interference when it launched its new test transmission on Eutelsat on 1 July. The station was not forced off air since it could still transmit using the Intelsat transponder. It is believed that only the Turkish government has the political motive, as well as the financial and technical capacity, to block Eutelsat. (MED-TV)

During a political demonstration on 29 July in Ankara, Turkish police assaulted eight journalists. They were: **Hayri Ozgur**, a cameraman for ATV; **Durak Dogan**, a cameraman for Kanal D; **Fevzi Gonulay**, a reporter for Ihlas news agency (IHA); **Cemalettin Alan**, a reporter for IHA: **Ismail Yesilyurt**, a reporter for Anatolian News Agency (ANA); **Mustafa Abada**, a reporter for ANA; and **Selahattin Sonmez**, a photographer for the *Turkish Daily News*. They were beaten by police with batons while covering a demonstration attended by Islamist and other activists. According to eyewitnesses, police officers were spurred on to attack the journalists at the urging of the crowd of demonstrators. (CPJ)

Eight editors have been released from prison following the unanimous passing of a limited amnesty law through parliament on 14 August, one month after incoming Prime Minister Mesut Yilmaz made a

public pledge to introduce greater press freedom. Included in the amnesty are **Ocak Isik Yurtcu, Bulent Balta** and **Mehmet Fatih Yesilbag** of *Ozgur Gundem*; **Mustafa Demirdag** of *Ozgur Gelecek*; **Naile Tuncer** of *Devrimci Proletarya*; and **Hatice Onaran** of *Devrimci Cozum*. The law suspends their jail terms for three years, but the sentences could be reactivated if a similar 'offence' were to be committed during the same period. A bill to extend the measure to include authors, writers, cartoonists and the other 75 journalists imprisoned under Turkey's Anti-Terror Law was rejected by deputies. (RSF)

UGANDA

Uganda Journalists Safety Committee (UJSC) has filed two constitutional petitions in the Constitutional Court seeking declarations that certain sections of the laws of sedition and the Press and Journalists Statute 1995 are unconstitutional. UJSC contends that the conviction and sentence of **Haruna Kanaabi** (*Index* 5/1995, 1&2/1996, 1/1997), editor of *Shariat,* were null and void and in violation of his constitutional rights. (Uganda Journalists Safety Committee)

UKRAINE

Alexej Kravchenko, editor-in-chief of the opposition newspaper *Vetcherniuj Sebastopol* was arrested on 24 June and sentenced to 10 days in prison for not respecting the decision of a court. He had refused to obey an order to print a reply from the Sebastopol mayor, **Viktor Sememov**, denying the accusations of corruption made in the paper in late 1996. *Vetcherniuj Sebastopol* was closed down on 24 June after authorities ordered the confiscation of its computers. An edition still appeared that day. (RSF)

Ukrainian deputy **Vladimir Alexeyev** told a news conference in Simferopol on 21 July that a draft law, under which Ukrainian would become the country's sole official language, had been submitted by the cabinet and president's office for approval by parliament. The bill proclaims Ukrainian the only idiom of communication in all social spheres, including in Crimea where 93 per cent of people are Russian-speakers. All civil servants and any person speaking another languages in a public office will be fined under the law.

Alexseyev condemned 'this coercive promotion of the Ukrainian language' as discrimination. Opposition parliamentary groups have prepared an alternative law, but the government version is more likely to be passed. (Reuters)

On 8 August **Konstiantyn Serdiuk**, editor-in-chief of *Chernihivskiy Pivden*, the independent Russian-language newspaper from the city of Chervihiv, was beaten up by three unknown assailants. He suffered brain damage and internal bleeding and is still in hospital. Journalists from the Chernihiv Media Club claimed that the attack was connected with a recent article by Serdiuk in which he criticised the local authorities. A screening of the satirical documentary 'An Ordinary President', about Belarusian President Alexander Luka-shenko, was recently banned

by the city council on the grounds that it interfered in the affairs of another country. (CPJ, RFE/RL)

Boris Derevyanko, editor-in-chief of the popular thrice-weekly newspaper *Vecgernyaya Odessa,* was shot dead on 11 August near the paper's offices in Odessa. Colleagues claim that his murder is related to the newspaper's criticism of the policies of Odessa's mayor, Eduard Gurvits, a former member of the USSR Supreme Soviet. Ruslan Bodelan, governor of the Odessa region, described the killing as an 'act of political terror'. Derevyanko's shooting is one in a series of attacks on journalists at *Vechernyaya Odessa*. In 1995 **Sergei Lebedev** survived an assassination attempt and, in the spring of this year, **Vitaly Chechik** was beaten by an assailant who told him to 'stop writing articles about the mayor.' Derevyanko was

---

• •

MARTÍN ESPADA

Another nameless prostitute

'I was a National Public Radio poet,' writes Martín Espada. 'In particular, I was an All Things Considered *poet. But now I've been censored because I wrote a poem about Mumia Abu-Jamal.' (For the case of Mumia Abu-Jamal see* Index *2/1996, 5/1996, 6/1996, 1/1997 and 3/1997.) In April 1997, Espada was commissioned by NPR to write a poem with a journalistic perspective. 'I read an article in the 16 April* Philadelphia Weekly,' *he writes in the* Progressive, *'describing a motion by one of Mumia's lawyers to introduce new testimony by an un-named prostitute. That became the catalyst for the poem. I also visited the tomb of Walt Whitman in nearby Camden.' Espada faxed the poem to NPR on 21 April. 'On 24 April,* All Things Considered *staff informed me that they would not air the poem because of its subject matter — Mumia Abu-Jamal — and its political sympathies. "NPR is refusing to air this poem because of its political content?" I asked. The reply: "Yes".'*

Another nameless prostitute
says the man is innocent

— *for Mumia Abu-Jamal, Philadelphia, PA/Camden, NJ, April 1997*

The board-blinded windows knew what happened;
the pavement sleepers of Philadelphia, groaning
in their ghost-infested sleep, knew what happened;
every black man blessed
with the gashed eyebrow of nightsticks
knew what happened;
even Walt Whitman knew what happened,
poet a century dead, keeping vigil
from the tomb on the other side of the bridge.

More than fifteen years ago,
the cataract stare of the cruiser's headlights,
the impossible angle of the bullet,
the tributaries and lakes of blood,
Officer Faulkner dead, suspect Mumia shot in the chest,
the witnesses who saw a gunman
running away, his heart and feet thudding.
The nameless prostitutes know,

• •

hunched at the curb, their bare legs chilled.
Their faces squinted to see that night,
rouged with fading bruises. Now the faces fade.
Perhaps an eyewitness putrefies eyes open in a bed of soil,
or floats in the warm gulf stream of her addiction,
or hides from the fanged whispers of the police
in the tomb of Walt Whitman,
where the granite door is open
and fugitive slaves may rest.

Mumia: the Panther beret, the thinking dreadlocks,
dissident words that swarmed the microphone like a hive,
sharing meals with people named Africa,
calling out their names even after the police bombardment
that charred their black bodies.
So the governor has signed the death warrant.
The executioner's needle would flush the poison
down into Mumia's writing hand
so the fingers curl like a burned spider;
his calm questioning mouth would grow numb,
and everywhere radios sputter to silence, in his memory.

The veiled prostitutes are gone, gone to the segregated balcony of whores.
But the newspaper reports that another nameless prostitute
says the man is innocent, that she will testify at the next hearing.
Beyond the courthouse, a multitude of witnesses chants, prays
shouts for his prison to collapse, a shack in a hurricane.

Mumia, if the last nameless prostitute
becomes an unravelling turban of steam,
if the judges's robes become clouds of ink
swirling like octopus deception,
if the shroud becomes your Amish quilt,
if your dreadlocks are snipped during autopsy,
then drift above the ruined RCA factory
that once birthed radios
to the tomb of Walt Whitman,
where the granite door is open
and fugitive slaves may rest.

Martín Espada *is author of five poetry collections, including* Imagine the Angels
of Bread *(WW Norton) which won the Before Columbus Foundation's American
Book Award*

beaten up in 1994, but was not thought to have received any recent threats. His funeral on 13 August was attended by more than 20,000 people. (RFE/RL)

UNITED KINGDOM

Schoolgirl **Sarah Briggs** was expelled from school in Mansfield, Notts, after complaining in a letter to a local newspaper of the high level of teacher absenteeism and poor teaching standards. The headteacher, Nicola Atkin, said she had brought the 'school into disrepute', and demanded an apology. When she refused, she was expelled in late July. Following a public outcry and criticism from the schools standards minister, she was re-instated and will resume studies in September. (*Independent, Guardian, The Times*)

An 11-year-old Protestant girl was forced on 12 July to remove her Spice Girls-style, Union Flag dress at a disco and change into a cardigan and jogging pants for fear of upsetting Catholics in Ballynahinch, Northern Ireland. Staff where the disco was held said they were concerned that the dress would cause a sectarian riot. The girl's parents were outraged and claim that the flag is not a political symbol. (*Guardian*)

On 13 August cameraman **Roddy Mansfield** was arrested while filming a protest against Rank Ltd's proposed clearing of Lyminage Forest in Kent. Mansfield was asked by a

member of the police tactical support group to recite from memory the PIN number on his National Union of Journalists press card, which also incorporates a laminated photograph. When he got the number wrong, his tapes were confiscated, he was hand-cuffed and then detained for three hours on charges of forging a press card. The story missed the bulletin deadlines for that day. (Undercurrents)

Recent publication: *An Agenda for Human Rights Protection (AI, June 1997, 10pp)*

URUGUAY

Individuals operating community radio stations could be punished with jail sentences of up to 10 years for a host of new crimes designed to protect the 'Nation, the State or its Powers... (and) the National Symbols'. The legislation was introduced in late July by the Partido Nacional, part of the coalition government, and also provides for a two-to-four year ban on the right to hold office, to participate in politics and vote, to carry out professional or academic work as well as the loss of 'parental authority'. (AMARC)

USA

The Amercian Civil Liberties Union filed a lawsuit against Oklahoma City on 4 July in response to police con-fiscation of copies of the 1979 film *The Tin Drum*. A judge had ruled that the film broke local pornography laws. (*Guardian, Independent on Sunday*)

On 10 August novelist **Paul Theroux** accused *Playboy* magazine of refusing to print extracts from his novel *Kowloon Tong,* in case it disrupted sales of their spin-off products in China. The novel is effectively banned in China, where Beijing's Office of Press and Publications has complained of its 'inaccurate depiction of mainland Chinese businessmen in Hong Kong, in particular...from the People's Liberation Army.' (*South China Morning Post*)

VENEZUELA

Journalist **William Ojeda** was pardoned and released from jail on 30 June after serving five months of a one-year sentence for defamation after publishing *How Much is a Judge Worth?*, an exposé of corruption in the legal system (*Index 2/1997*). (IFJ/FIP)

VIETNAM

On 20 August the government announced plans to tighten censorship controls on foreign films. The move, partly aimed at protecting the domestic film industry, is also intended to crack down on illegal video distribution networks, through which banned foreign films and pornography are freely available on the black market. (Reuters)

WESTERN SAMOA

On 9 July the Supreme Court forbade the *Samoa Observer* from reporting allegations about the management of the government-owned Poly-nesian Airlines. The following morning, the paper left part of its front page blank in protest. The court order is the latest government move against the island's leading independent newspaper. On 20 June Prime Minister Tofilau Eti Alesana threatened to remove the paper's business licence because it had been 'stirring up trouble'. (Pacific Islands News Association)

ZAMBIA

The government appealed to the Supreme Court on 17 July against the release from jail of **Fred M'membe** and **Bright Mwape**, editor-in-chief and managing editor of the privately-owned newspaper the *Post*. The two were jailed 'indefinitely' in February last year for 'contempt of parliament' (*Index* 2/1996, 3/1996, 4/1996, 5/1996, 6/1996). They were released after 24 days by Supreme Court judge Kabazo Chanda. The next appeal hearing has been set for 9 October. On 5

August the High Court granted finance minister Ronald Penza an injunction preventing the *Post* from publishing allegations against him of corruption. (MISA)

Masautso Phiri, the *Post*'s special projects editor, was arrested for taking pictures at the 23 August opposition rally in Kabwe where former president Kenneth Kaunda was wounded in the head in what he later alleged was an assassination attempt. Phiri, whose work has led to frequent confrontations with the authorities, had his cameras smashed, his film destroyed and suffered an assault. He was released on 25 August, but refused to pay the K6,000 (US$5) 'duty of admission', whereby he would not be required to appear in court. A hearing to decide whether Phiri caused a breach of the peace was fixed for 3 September. (MISA, *Post*)

★★★

General publications: *Nurses and Human Rights* (AI, June 1997, 21pp); *The Death Penalty Worldwide: Developments in 1996* (AI, June 1997, 19pp); *Fear, Flight and Forcible Exile: Refugees in the Middle East* (AI, September 1997, 27pp); *Famine Crimes: Politics & the Disaster Relief Industry in Africa* by Alex de Waal (African Rights & International African Institute in association with James Currey & Indiana University Press, 1997, 238pp); *The International Criminal Court: Making the Right Choices — Part II* (AI, July 1997, 92pp)

★★★

Compiled by: Nikolai Hutchinson (Africa); Andrew Kendle, Nicky Winstanley-Torode, Sarah A Smith (Asia); Mathew Little, Vera Rich (eastern Europe & CIS); Susan Casey (Latin America); Michaela Becker, Rupert Clayton (Middle East); Stephen Geesing (north America & Pacific); Nevine Mabro (western Europe)

Harold Pinter, *Index on Censorship* & the Almeida Theatre present

Look, Europe!

A staged reading of a new play by Ghazi Rabihavi

cast includes

Rhydian Jones
Harold Pinter
Nadim Sawalha
Christopher Simon

Directed by Gari Jones

At the Almeida Theatre, London on Sunday 5 October

I am writing down this account in great haste in the hope that people one day will be able to read it, and that the world, the Iranian public and not least my wife and my children, whom I love most intensely, will discover what a terrible ordeal I have been dragged into.

Faraj Sarkoohi, editor of the independent literary magazine *Adineh*, wrote these words on 3 January 1997, during a brief period of freedom granted him by the Ministry of Intelligence in Iran. The letter, smuggled out of the country, described how his captors had forced him to incriminate himself as a spy.

Sarkoohi's trial continues, in camera, despite the efforts of Western organisations to secure a public trial and legal assistance. His open letter was a will and testament, and a bold exposure by a journalist outside whose prison cell death is pacing.

Index author Ghazi Rabihavi has written a powerful and moving play about his colleague and compatriot. Proceeds from the performance will support *Index*'s associated charity Writers & Scholars Educational Trust.

Tickets are on sale from the Almeida box office, price £15 and £10.

Almeida Theatre, Almeida Street, London N11TA
Telephone 0171 359 4404